The Art of
Peaceful Teaching
in the Primary School

Improving Behaviour and Preserving Motivation

Michelle MacGrath

2

David Fulton Publishers

David Fulton Publishers
2 Park Square, Milton Park, Abingdon, Oxon OX14 4RN

270 Madison Avenue, New York, NY 10016

First published in Great Britain by David Fulton Publishers 2000
Transferred to digital printing

*David Fulton Publishers is an imprint of the Taylor & Francis Group, an informa
business*

British Library Cataloguing in Publication Data

A catalogue record for this book is available from the British Library.

ISBN 1–85346–654–9

Typeset by Textype Typesetters, Cambridge

Contents

Acknowledgements

Many people have generously contributed to this book. I would especially like to thank my partner, David Mann, for all his love and support, and our sons, Mark and Peter, for their sense of fun and for helping me learn. I would also like to thank Valerie Phillips for her care and truthfulness.

Particular thanks for their written contributions, interviews, material and discussions to Gillian Backhouse, Charlie Beer, Mark Davelle, Mikaela Davies, Lucy Davis, Susan House, Lesley Morris, Liz Murphy, Linda Reade, Sheila Stone and Debbie Swyer. They retain the copyright for their work.

Thanks also for their help and support to Susan and Peter Bloomfield, Tony Brown, Julia Clark, Don Clarke, Anne Dickson, Chantal Howell, Vladimir Levi, Dorothy Lewis, Michael Marland, Linda Marsh, Janine Mather, Susannah McInerney, Anne Murray, Kathy Naire, Khaleghl Quinn, Jiffy Sandison, Juliette Stephenson, Felicity Yates and all the children and colleagues with whom I have worked.

Children learn what they live

If a child lives with criticism,
he learns to condemn.
If a child lives with hostility,
he learns to fight.
If a child lives with ridicule,
he learns to be shy.
If a child lives with shame,
he learns to feel guilty.
If a child lives with tolerance,
he learns to be patient.
If a child lives with encouragement,
he learns confidence.
If a child lives with praise,
he learns to appreciate.
If a child lives with fairness,
he learns justice.
If a child lives with security,
he learns to have faith.
If a child lives with approval,
he learns to like himself.
If a child lives with acceptance and friendship,
he learns to find love in the world.

NSPCC 1990

To David and our sons, Mark and Peter,
and to children and their teachers everywhere.

Introduction

Observe most children of 3, 4, or 5 and you will notice how curious they are. Place them in a novel environment, for example, on a first visit to a friend's house and they will, sooner or later, and often quite systematically, set about exploring the new toys at hand. Most children are also able, without undue difficulty, to acquire language and take risks in applying it in different situations. Many can sit and listen for sustained periods of time to their favourite stories or concentrate on a task they find captivating. Indeed, young children are naturally well equipped to find out about the world around them, to test out their theories and experiment since humans have always needed these skills for survival. Considering all this, it would seem that there would be little need to motivate children to learn in school. Indeed, in many situations, it would be difficult to *stop* them from learning. However, this is frequently not the case. The Keele University survey (Centre for Successful Schools, 1994) carried out among secondary pupils found that over a fifth of pupils considered their work boring and almost a third would prefer not to go to school. Clearly, there has been considerable change since the time when most children enthusiastically started school, namely a considerable number of children stop wanting to learn, or, to be precise, stop wanting to learn *in school*.

Although this survey deals with pupils of secondary age, primary school teachers cannot afford to ignore the issue since, for some young people, the process of demoralisation and disaffection begins during their time in primary. This may not manifest itself as disruptive behaviour or overt aggression in school, but there may be, for example, a loss of excitement in learning, boredom, growing cynicism, diminishing confidence and self-esteem, a ceasing to try or to care about others' opinions, or just mild uncooperativenss.

Undoubtedly there are wider issues here about the overall aims and structure of education which go beyond the scope of this book. Individual teachers cannot singlehandedly change an entire system, yet, what they can do is very valuable. Namely, they can analyse the process of what goes on in their classrooms in order to develop the best practice possible for preserving and activating motivation. In a sense, this is almost the most important task facing the primary teacher: how can he or she create the conditions in which *all* pupils can develop and refine their skills in learning, thinking and understanding and can actively desire to do so.

The aim of the book is to support creative thinking and confidence in the reader since, with these two attributes, the classroom teacher is best placed to find his or her own solutions to the various challenges and difficulties of teaching. The technique is to present a collage of differing ideas, suggestions, examples and experience which might resonate with the reader.

The first two chapters consider ways of avoiding disaffection and promoting motivation. These issues are interrelated, rather like two sides of a coin and some material could have been included in either chapter. The distinction between preserving motivation and avoiding disaffection is often a very subjective one. The third chapter considers the role of relationships, standing as they do at the very heart of teaching. It looks at ways of developing good enough working relationships with children and parents and helping children to work and play cooperatively with each other. An essential aspect of building relationships which function well is the ability to manage conflict and anger, one's own and that of others. This forms the focus of Chapter 4. Troublesome behaviour can demand considerable time and energy from the class teacher. Depending on how it is handled, it can detract from everyone's sense of enjoyment in learning and serve as a demoralising factor for all, or it can become an opportunity for everyone to learn. Chapter 5 suggests constructive approaches to avoiding and dealing with troublesome behaviour which aim to build self-esteem, cooperation and motivation. The final chapter is aimed at supporting the teacher's own well-being and sense of satisfaction.

This book is about the process of helping children learn and what they need in order to do this. It may sometimes seem overwhelming to have to think about the process of learning in great detail when dealing with the demands of getting across the body of content embedded in a curriculum, yet it is crucial for two reasons. Firstly, if you cannot find a way through to the children and work *with* them then, although you might have delivered the curriculum, they will not have benefited from it. Secondly, facts are not a scarcity. Quite the reverse, young people today are bombarded with information of all kinds. Acquiring data is, in a sense, less of a challenge for young people than being able to discriminate, think about and use the mass of information they have at their fingertips, working collaboratively with others or alone as most appropriate.

It is already clear that the demands of the twenty-first century will be very different from those of the twentieth and will require a different preparation for adult life. As the business world has found out, skills are needed which are not always developed in schools: for example, the ability to collaborate, interact with others and accept feedback. Since these are not subjects but life skills, they can in fact be developed through the medium of the curriculum if the process is one which is sensitive to individual needs, involves active learning and is based on mutual respect and shared objectives. In other words, if it is a process which enables children to learn how to learn and think efficiently, a process which intrinsically develops confidence, self-esteem and communication and social skills and which excites and satisfies children sufficiently to want to carry on learning. The question for the primary teacher is *how* to do this, that is to say, what kind of process will best achieve these ends?

Primary teachers are an amazing resource of creativity, professional skills and energy. The ideas, strategies and thinking in this book are given for teachers to shape and develop in their own way to fit their personal style and particular circumstances. Educational theories have a tendency to come and go with a certain regularity. What remains is the relationship between the teacher and the pupils and the immense learning potential of each child. The aim of this book is to help new, unconfident, disillusioned or enquiring teachers to find their own ways of seeing, hearing and meeting the thirty or so individuals in their class, unlocking their learning potential and maintaining the children's innate excitement at learning.

Chapter 1

Avoiding disaffection

For me it would be progress to live in a culture with less humiliation.
  (Adam Phillips, psychotherapist, *In Our Time*, Radio 4, 18 November 1999)

What do children need in order to learn? As one primary teacher put it, *'You can't have progress unless a child is happy. Happiness and progress go hand in hand.'* This may seem a little excessive since it is obviously impossible to ensure the happiness of all the children in the class. Yet what the teacher said is also true: unless pupils are comfortable in the classroom, unless they have friends and are happy enough with the relationships in the class and unless they feel sufficiently at ease in the school they will not learn. In other words, unless their emotional well-being is considered progress will be severly hampered: children's feelings count.

A teacher of English as an Additional Language found a startling difference in one pupil over the course of a few months. The first term she worked with her the girl had been uncooperative, surly and uncommunicative, even though her spoken English was more than adequate. During the second term, however, she changed dramatically, beginning to cooperate, working hard, being friendly towards the teacher and making good progess with her written English. When the teacher asked her what had changed and why she was now so different, the girl was very clear, saying, 'The first term I was all alone in the world. I knew no one. Now I have my friend Shamsun. Now I have everything.'

Powerful emotions of any kind interfere with concentration as anyone who has sat an exam, been distracted after a fierce argument or just fallen in love would probably testify. It is sometimes easy as adults to underestimate how important relationships are to children who have neither the life experience to put disagreements or difficulties into perspective nor the same possibilities of moving freely into different groups seeking new friendships. Many lack the social and communication skills to sort out disagreements unaided. Time is never wasted by teachers when it is spent on developing relationships and cultivating the capacity of young people to manage them effectively.

The groundwork for any academic achievement is, therefore, the far more intangible task of helping children feel comfortable enough with themselves, the rest of the class and the teacher in order to be able to apply themselves to school work. Of course, they also need to be able to manage tasks set, contribute to discussions and feel successful as students in order to feel good about themselves.

Emotional well-being and success at school are thus inextricably linked.

Tom Bentley (1998), refers to pupils as 'intelligent agents'. In other words, children have to be active participants in their own learning and development rather than passive objects, 'empty vessels' to be filled with knowledge. Although there will always be a body of knowledge with which children need to become acquainted, this is best encompassed in an approach which encourages independence, decision-making and responsibility. The very meaning of the word 'educate', to lead out, suggests a journey in which young people are equipped with the necessary skills and supported in their development from the richness of their own inner world to the world at large. While the curriculum forms the content of this journey it is the form, the process through which that is assimilated which will help equip children with the skills they will need to flourish in the adult world. Process is crucial and is the subject of this book.

Certainly two things are today clear. Firstly, we live in an information society in which children have access to more data more easily than ever before. Many, for example, will not only have absorbed information about other countries from watching television, but will actually have travelled or even lived there. In other words, children come to school with not only opinions, preferences and aptitudes but sometimes also considerable knowledge: the world at large can now impinge on a child's inner world at a very young age. Secondly, young people themselves are very aware that they are responsible for their own learning and that no one can make them learn. In a recent MORI survey in Britain it was found that 67 per cent of 11–16-year-olds agreed with the statement that *'No one can make you learn, you have to want to learn'*.

Consequently, unless, as teachers, we truly acknowledge the children's role as active participants through the approach we take and the kinds of activities we use we will run the risk of demotivating some children and simply appearing irrelevant to others, thereby creating conditions which will lead to behaviour difficulties now or in the future. Schooling in the West has to compete with the excitement of virtual reality games, the immediacy of the internet the shifting colours and sounds of television and the constant bombardment of advertising. Paper and pencil, flip chart and blackboard are, perhaps, less immediately appealing to many than these accompaniments to modern life. That is probably true without the element of the teacher since, ultimately, it is the human element, the fun and support of relationships, feeling liked, valued and accepted, the opportunity of choosing and being creative, the sense of growing independence and responsibility, the security of belonging to a group and the satisfaction of achievement which are the most sustaining motivators of all. The question for the teacher is how to do all this? What is required to sustain motivation and enable children to perceive themselves as and to become able, willing and independent students? What can extend their depth of understanding, widen their scope of interests and add to and refine their skills? A place to start is for the teacher to:

- find ways into learning which will engage every child;
- help children develop their own strategies for learning and reflection;
- develop sustaining relationships;

- help children feel good about themselves and happy enough in school in order to learn.

This book aims to suggest ways of thinking and practical strategies which will enable teachers to achieve this more of the time. One place to start is to consider how to establish the kind of environment which will promote learning.

1. Establishing a calm and purposeful environment

It is no contradiction that, in order to allow pupils as much independence and responsibility as possible regarding their work, it is usually helpful to develop a structure which is ordered and routine. This is particularly useful for those pupils who are most insecure, for whatever reason, and who, therefore, are most likely to disrupt the activities of the class. Even though they will have choice and independence in some areas of their work they will thus feel contained by the structure you have established and, consequently, more at ease in the classroom. The more children know what to expect regarding the order and procedures of the day, the more relaxed they will feel and the more emotional energy they will have to channel towards work. You will also be less troubled with questions about what is to happen in the future. It is usually useful to remember that what may seem obvious to an adult probably will not to a child, so often it is necessary to state details very clearly, checking the children have understood and writing up important information.

In order for pupils to work independently and effectively they will also need help in developing essential skills such as resolving conflict, working collaboratively, reflecting on work, discriminating, listening to others, sitting quietly and so on. Most of these skills will be developed through the process in which the content of the curriculum is conveyed.

As the teacher you are in charge: it is up to you to minimise opportunities for disaffection in your class. One way of doing so is through providing relevant, accessible, engaging and interesting activities for the children and this is considered in the following chapter. Another way is to organise your classroom procedures in such a way that there are few chances for children to start chatting, playing, fighting or behaving in a way you do not wish them to. Such a strategy will instantly avoid a considerable amount of 'telling off' which can lead to resentment and disaffection. Useful techniques include:

- Routine procedures, for example:
  - a procedure for entering the school building and classroom and sitting down
  - a strategy for giving things out and packing away
  - an ordered procedure for leaving the class, by table, by row, etc.
  - efficient personal organisation;
- a seating plan;
- a quick start to activities;
- only purposeful to-ing and fro-ing during activities;
- clear expectations;

- rewards for good behaviour;
- consistent consequences for poor behaviour;
- training in how to sit quietly, listen, etc.

Let us consider some of these in more detail. Further relevant information can be found in the section 'Helping a whole class to change' towards the end of Chapter 5.

Entering the building and the classroom

In the playground children will be involved in a range of activities: walking, talking loudly, running, shouting, playing a game, playing football, fighting, and so on. These are activities which are obviously inappropriate inside the school building. If the children are allowed to enter the building from the playground unsupervised and in a disorderly fashion it can cause difficulties later on. Cloakrooms are an area where there can be considerable jostling and confusion. There may be shoving and pushing in corridors or on stairs which can lead to arguments or fights. These are sometimes taken into the classroom and set the tone for the day. Order established early on avoids these unnecessary tussles. The doorway marks the divide between free play and more purposeful activity. Another way of looking at it is that, when the children take off their coats, they leave any vestiges of playground behaviour in the cloakroom or on the hook. It can wait for them there until they go outside again to play or go home.

If the teacher leads the children in from outside he or she can help them to quieten and calm down before leaving the playground. This is usually easier if the children are made aware of standing differently: straight and still, looking ahead. A change in body posture can often help children alter behaviour more quickly than if they are given an order to stop talking, stop fidgeting, etc. Another way of creating a change of mood quickly is to engage the children's interest and imagination about the forthcoming tasks by setting them a puzzle or question to think about on their way to class.

It can also be very helpful if the pupils know exactly what to do when they enter the classroom. That is to say, they know where to go and sit and they have something they can do straight away. For example, they may put their folders in a box, and sit in their seats reading their ongoing class reader. Or, having put away their folders, they may sit on the mat quietly working out a puzzle the teacher has put on the board. Without such a strategy, unwanted behaviour is more likely. Those children who are most insecure tend to find unstructured times like these periods of transition most difficult to handle and, consequently, often start some unwanted behaviour. This might lead to the teacher intervening and telling them off and the pattern for the day is set. With these children in particular it is generally helpful if the first contact each day is a welcome from you rather than a comment in response to some inappropriate behaviour.

There are other advantages to having a routine activity for pupils on entering in a morning. One of these is that the children start off the day independently, that is to say, they come in knowing what to do and are able to take responsibility for doing so without instructions or with very little comment from the teacher. If a parent needs to speak with the teacher urgently at this time the children are not left waiting. Latecomers can also be absorbed without disruption to others. The first coming together, sharing and instructions for the rest of the day may come after five or ten minutes of quiet, independent activity. If such a start is impractical first thing it could be employed on returning to class after lunch and used as a way to help pupils calm down and refocus on work.

Ending a session and leaving the class

The end of each session is, in a sense, the beginning of the next one since it often gives the pupil an impression he or she will remember. In other words, if the ending is slightly chaotic with children wandering out of class chatting, this is likely to feed their expectations of how they can behave with you at your next meeting. Similarly, if the ending is one characterised by conflict or criticism pupils may well be a little unwilling to return for more of the same. It is, therefore, usually helpful to end each day and each week on a positive note, even when things have been difficult, by emphasising what has been achieved, and maybe even enjoyed, and looking forward to working together next time. *If the children generally leave your class feeling good about themselves, good about what they have achieved and optimistic for the future they will usually be keen to come back.*

Efficient personal organisation

The primary day is filled with a multitude of small demands and difficulties which can easily upset the smooth running of an activity and take up teacher time: broken pencils, for example, lost books, paper not available, biros running out, arguments about whose turn it is to go on the computer or to take the register to the office, and so on. Therefore, the more a teacher can streamline his or her personal organisation, the more energy and time he or she will have for helping children learn. Such detailed strategies as careful record-keeping, a rota for turns on the computer and for class jobs, a tray of pencil sharpeners into which children sharpen their pencils and which is cleaned out by pencil monitors who also care for pots of coloured pencils for each table, a treasure box into which precious items brought to show the class are kept safe during the day, a notebook for jotting down urgent tasks for the day, things to remember and good ideas for the future can all ease the practicalities of a busy day.

It is usually helpful to decide on a policy for allowing children to go to the toilet since requests for this can cause confusion. Not to allow children to go at all is unwise since accidents may happen and if children are concerned about this they will be unable to concentrate on their work. Some ground rules are, therefore, helpful. One teacher employs the following policy and finds that it works well. The children write their names on a small piece of card and pin this onto a red board. When they wish to go to the toilet they take their name and place it on the green board which is beside the red one. Only two children are allowed out of the room at any one time. When they return, they replace their name on the red board. This system means that, at any time, the teacher can see who is out of the room and can, therefore notice any patterns which may form, for example, a pupil always going to the toilet directly after a break, or two children frequently being out of the class at the same time. If such patterns occur the teacher can then talk to the pupils involved. Mostly, however, the system makes no particular demands on the teacher at all. It also gives the children a degree of responsibility and autonomy which ensures that most of them will respect the system most of the time.

A seating plan

A well-devised seating plan can avoid difficulties almost more than any other single strategy. There are several point to consider.

- How and where do you want the desks?
- What is best for small group work?
- What also allows pupils to see the board?
- Who works well with whom?
- Who might chatter or otherwise distract others?
- Who might need extra help with language, numeracy or literacy?
- Where is your desk?
- Where are the pupils who demand most attention?

Some children work best with their friends, some do not since they are too distracted by talking or playing together. If friendship groups are split up, however, this can sometimes lead to resentment, becoming yet one more reason why some children are demotivated and dislike school. One way to forestall this is to discuss with the children the idea of working partnerships rather than friendships. This is, in fact, like the world of work: few friends start a job working together; most become friends through the process of working together. If the children understand that there are different kinds of relationships, that they might enjoy playing with one person, but prefer working with another, it can often help them accept seating plans. Often children themselves will be aware of who it is best for them to sit next to and work with.

The presence of the teacher can be a powerful force. Where the teacher stands and sits is, therefore, of some importance. I was asked to observe a girl in Year 2. The teacher felt very despondent regarding her and thought she was never on task and always distracted. After observing the class for some time it was clear that, whenever the teacher was near her, the girl worked on her task. This was true even when the teacher was facing in the other direction attending to someone else: it was the teacher's presence alone that spurred the pupil on to purposeful activity. Consequently, it was only when the teacher was in another part of the room that the pupil stopped working and started to chat and distract her neighbours.

A quick start

As the teacher it is easy to become annoyed if children keep you waiting when you are ready to begin an activity. Other children can become restless and distractions start. Similarly, it is useful to be well prepared so that, if possible, you do not keep the class waiting for you to be ready.

Additional activities

There will always be children finishing tasks at different times. One way to ensure pupils are never left, unsure of what to do next, is to have two or three ongoing tasks they know they can choose to work on when they have finished the class work. This might be reading, a journal to write, a piece of sewing, sketching a still life, book-making, craft activities, and so on. The important thing is that the task is one which children can do independently, one that they enjoy doing, and one that it is possible to complete by working on it five minutes here and there. Some ideas for activities for those children who work well and finish quickly can be found in Chapter 5 (see page 133 'Maintaining motivation').

Enjoyment and choice are important here since, in a sense, these activites can be seen as 'rewards' for having finished work early to a high standard. If simply more work is given it can be a disincentive to some children to finish. For example, even when he was in reception one boy was affected by this and developed a very slow way of working in school in order to avoid what he saw as extra work. It was noticeable that, at home, he always completed any writing he chose to do very quickly. The habit he had developed at primary school could, however, seriously hinder his achievement, particularly once he was working at secondary level. As this example illustrates, it is usually worth questioning what we are training children to do by the process and activities we set up in the classroom.

Purposeful to-ing and fro-ing

Disruptive behaviour frequently occurs when children are out of their seats. They may be legitimately on their way to collect equipment or to see the teacher when passing a friend, or an 'enemy', proves to be too much of a temptation and they start chatting, give a passing punch or make a comment, etc. Or they may be at a loose end because the work is too difficult, because they are tired or bored or want to stretch their legs. Whatever the reason, wandering around the classroom can lead to unwanted behaviour. Yet it is also unreasonable to expect children to sit still for up to two hours without moving around from time to time. Some techniques follow which can help minimise disruption caused by to-ing and fro-ing.

- If possible, ensure that equipment is accessible and that children have it on their desk or can get it without bumping into classmates.
- Train the class to take mini-breaks when they feel tired or want to move about. This might consist of tensing the whole body, counting to three and then relaxing slowly from the head down. This is to be done three times before stretching, yawning silently and returning to the activity in hand.
- Discuss how it is best for everyone to move around: for example, leaving their seat only when necessary; taking the most direct route; walking quietly; returning to their seat as soon as possible.

Clear expectations: developing cooperation

The experience of being in a classroom organised around the rules a teacher has set often feels very different from one in which the children have had a part in formulating expectations for behaviour. This is true for everyone involved. While the rules and expectations themselves may be similar, the process by which they have been established is very different. Rules can become a focus for disagreement, a battleground in which time and energy are lost and relationships become soured. This is often because they appear to the children to be arbitrary, senseless, a means of stopping fun and imposed from above. If children are not consulted and have no part in drawing up a code of behaviour they are less likely to have a personal investment in abiding by it since it has little meaning for them. They may not understand why rules are important other than because the teacher says they are. If, however, the children can play an active part in devising a class code they will have to do the work of thinking which expectations are helpful to them and why. That is to say, the points in the code do not belong to the teachers but to them, the children. Often they will help each other keep the code.

The details of how to develop a class code cooperatively would vary depending on the age of the pupils involved. Here are three suggestions.

1. The teacher asks the children in groups of 3 or 4 to decide on 5 or 6 expectations of behaviour that would most help them learn. Ideas are then pooled and discussed further. As the teacher, you know what you need in order to feel comfortably in charge and for the class to run smoothly. If the children omit anything essential the teacher can introduce it into the discussion or direct their attention to a general area they may have missed, for example, expectations for how you speak and listen to others. Most classes, with some guidance perhaps, will come up with a code which is practical.

   The teacher may also wish to draw attention to the wording of rules so that the desired behaviour is emphasised, since this focuses on *doing* something rather than on *not doing* or stopping something. It is often easier, for example, to sit quietly than to stop talking since your attention is drawn to the target behaviour rather than to what is to be stopped. The children may need encouragement to be as specific as possible or to discuss what is meant exactly by a term. Consequently, a discussion of examples of how to be 'kind, considerate and helpful' could help the class and the teacher more closely share expectations about behaviour.

   Once the class code has been drawn up pupils decide how they would most like to display it. What would help them keep the expectations in mind? A prominent display is usually most effective, although the children might also want their own copy or maybe a class book of pictures and comments. After a time it can be useful to assess the efficiency of the code. Does anything need to be changed or added and why? A class may well wish to take their code with them from year to year. A new teacher might like to review it with the children to see what is still relevant and what may need altering as they grow and develop. New children entering the class could be given their own copy of the code, a classmate explaining it to them.

2. A more structured way of including the children in drawing up a class code is for the teacher to provide a list of expectations, perhaps based on the school behaviour policy, and to ask the class in pairs or small groups to rank them in

order of importance. What can most help them to learn and to enjoy their time in the classroom? By discussing the relative merits of points in the code the pupils are involved in assessing the need for agreed behaviours which ultimately help them.

3. Another approach is to discuss a list of expectations with the class, eliciting from them the wording they would like. Again this gives them an active part in the process, helping them to own the expectations and to make sense of them.

    Although this process will take some time in the short term, overall it will save considerable time, effort and aggravation since the code is endorsed by the children themselves. If the school as a whole is open to this approach it could be possible for all classes to participate in drawing up a code of behaviour for the playground too. Playtime staff can then be involved in the discussion.

It remains the task of the teacher to maintain boundaries firmly and kindly. Without this the classroom would be unsafe both physically and emotionally. Those children who are most insecure find a lack of such boundaries frightening. As a result, they are more likely to resort to increasingly extreme behaviour in order to 'push' the teacher into setting a limit. A few thoughtful expectations of behaviour contribute to the overall physical and emotional safety of the classroom. They help create a calmer atmosphere without which many children will not feel comfortable enough to engage in any creative endeavour. Maintaining boundaries may at times involve some quick thinking and flexibility concerning the essence of the instruction and a compromise in order for both parties to save face.

For example, a girl in Year 2 was asked to throw away some scraps of paper she was still holding after clearing up. She refused. The teacher was surprised since the girl usually complied, but she thought quickly. Realising that the girl might want to show the scraps to her parents, she suggested she gave them to her to look after till home time. In this way, the teacher thought of a *third solution* which avoided confrontation while still maintaining her authority in the eyes of the rest of the class. The girl was also able to accept the teacher's authority since she could do so without backing down. Both were in fact satisfied: the pupil did not throw the paper in the bin; the teacher ensured that no one on the mat was holding scraps of paper. Both had saved face. If the teacher had assumed that the girl was trying to defy her or if she had become fixed on the idea that the paper had to go into the bin, rather than that the girl no longer held it on the mat, the incident would probably have ended in conflict.

It is useful to get clear in your own mind what is essential to you and on what points you can be more flexible since this helps convey a sense of confidence. Ultimately it is our own internal clarity about what is acceptable and what is not which lends confidence to any requests or demands we make. *In other words, it is to our own inner authority that children will respond.* However thorough you might be in this preparation, there are likely to be times when you have to question and confirm your limits on the spot.

It is also useful to question what is the essence of our demand. In the example above, it was that the girl was not holding the paper rather than that she threw it in the bin. In the heat of the moment it is easy to get stuck on one demand as the only possible course of action, thinking we must be obeyed, particularly if we assume a child is being deliberately defiant. More often than not, *to begin with* he or she has another agenda, as in this case. If, however, the teacher instantly treats a child as if he or she is defiant then conflict is likely. The role of a teacher's expectations are discussed in more detail in Chapter 3.

Sitting still

Children like and need to move. Depending on their ways of thinking and learning, some will need to do so more than others. The demands of the infant curriculum in particular will be difficult for many to meet since they are still at an age when moving around the classroom learning through play is more appropriate than sitting on the mat or at desks for long periods at a time. It can, therefore, sometimes be a fine line between training pupils to sit still and making an age-inappropriate demand on some children. What can the teacher do in this situation?

In any class there is often a wide range of ability as far as sitting still is concerned. Some pupils will be able to remain fairly still for sustained periods of time if they are absorbed in something interesting, listening to a favourite story, for example, painting a picture or doing a puzzle. Others in the same class are likely to have a very short attention span and will start fidgeting, sprawling, annoying a neighbour or wandering around the classroom after a very short amount of time. This can present a challenge to most teachers since such behaviour can be very distracting for others. It can be helpful to remain very sensitive to the individual child, noting who finds sitting still particularly difficult and considering strategies which might work for him or her. It is often more constructive to perceive fidgeting and moving about as a child's inability to sit or stand still through lack of practice, physiological state or developmental stage rather than as a conscious attempt to disobey or behave 'badly'.

One strategy that can work with young children is to brainstorm with them the names of three or four animals or birds which sit quietly, still and alert, cats, for example, or owls, or rabbits. Once these have been discussed, the children then choose the creature which they will imitate when asked to sit still and quiet. The children might sometimes sit on the mat in their animal group. In this way, pupils can use their imaginations to practise a particular posture which can help them concentrate. Older children might like to choose role models from famous historical characters, Queen Victoria, perhaps, or Neil Armstrong.

Obviously, the more interesting activities are and the more they involve pupils the less likely they are to become distracted and to distract others. Likewise, it can be helpful to plan a range of activities so that there are not extended periods of sitting still listening. For example, if the class has just returned from a long assembly where they have been expected to sit quietly then a different kind of activity would probably be wise.

Another approach is to incorporate movement into or between activities for young children. This can be particularly useful for those children who learn best through moving, touching and doing. Some ideas are included in the next chapter for using movement in learning sounds and letter and number shapes. PE can be a time when movement and stillness are explicitly explored. The aim is to help children become aware of when and how they move and, as a contrast, how it feels to be as still as possible. This transition from movement to stillness can be practised regularly. Before a period of sitting still in class the children might be asked to move consciously for a short time, for example, jumping on the spot. From this period of movement they then change to sitting very still as practised in PE. The use of mini-breaks suggested earlier might also be helpful for some children who need to move frequently.

Listening

It is of tremendous benefit if children are aware of how to listen attentively early on in their school career. Many children can listen well as long as their interest is held, although some who are accustomed only to watching TV and rarely listening to stories may find it harder to concentrate on listening alone without watching. The length of attention span, will vary hugely in any class. The aim is to help children to stay focused for longer and to be able to return to listening quickly when their attention wanders. Training in listening skills can be integrated into the day as regular five-minute activities. Some suggestions to consider are:

- ensure that the content is as interesting, relevant and accessible as possible;
- sometimes use guided listening, that is to say, explain to the children beforehand and write up for them anything in particular you are asking them to listen out for; the greater need they have to find out something, the better they will listen;
- ask the children to adopt a 'listening position', a sitting position which will help them listen carefully; this may be the position they would be in to listen to something they find extremely interesting; whenever you are asking them to listen, remind them to adopt their special posture; they may need one position for listening on the mat and one for sitting at their tables;
- practise, sometimes as a game, sometimes in small groups or pairs, as well as with a whole class;
- discuss difficulties they have in staying focused and on track; what is the difference between hearing and listening? When do they stop listening and how do they know when they have stopped?

Some listening games can be found in Appendices B.

2. Helping children develop relevant skills

The skills referred to earlier which underly a sense of both emotional well-being and a perception of oneself as a successful student are essential not only in school but also in life. They are the skills which help people, whether it is managing in difficult situations or building a fulfilling career or relationship. Teaching which does not help pupils develop these skills will also ultimately lead to disaffection since children will experience a gulf between what is useful to them in the 'real' world and what they are taught at school. These skills can be developed by involving pupils as 'intelligent agents' in their own learning and by helping them acquire and refine relevant social and communication skills. Reference to this occurs throughout the book.

3. Building confidence and self-esteem

A good enough degree of confidence and self-esteem is essential if a child is to develop his or her potential. Without this any amount of knowledge can prove of little value in dealing with life. It is, therefore, very helpful if the question underlying all our classroom management and teaching strategies is that of whether they build or undermine confidence and self-esteem. These terms are frequently used, but not always considered or defined in detail. Yet the clearer we are about what they are and how they are gained the more effective we can be in helping children develop them. Confidence and self-esteem are often interrelated and complement each other: with very poor self-esteem, for example, it is more difficult to gain confidence in any field; whereas increased confidence and the praise and acceptance this may win can sometimes help raise self-esteem.

Confidence is often referred to in connection with a specific skill. You can be confident in some areas of your life and unconfident in others. For example, you can be a confident cyclist, but unconfident at singing. Let us think a little about how confidence is built. Some of the essential elements seem to be gained by:

- actually doing something;
- succeeding enough of the time; children with very poor confidence and self-esteem will need to succeed all the time or they are likely to give up; as children develop more confidence and their self-esteem improves, they are able to manage greater challenges and even failure, if they are given sufficient support;
- being encouraged;
- your endeavour being acknowledged;
- meeting your own and others' expectations;
- developing independence;
- managing responsibility.

Self-esteem is more general in scope since it concerns how we perceive ourselves, often in relation to others. It is developed largely through relationships by:

- feeling accepted for who you are;
- feeling loved;
- feeling liked;
- feeling one of a group;
- feeling valued.

In any one class you will encounter some children confident in many areas and others confident in few, some with high and others with low self-esteem. Teaching involves accepting every child unconditionally while he or she is in your class and building his or her confidence and self-esteem in every way you can.

4. Common causes of disaffection and some alternative strategies

In a sense, anything which undermines the conditions above can easily contribute to disaffection, in other words, anything which undermines the pupils' emotional well-being or their sense of themselves as able and eager students who have a part to play in their own learning. This is not to say a teacher cannot tell pupils off, maintain boundaries firmly and carry through sanctions if necessary, since this may well be required at some point. However, the question is *how* to maintain order in such a way as to build or at least not undermine pupils' self-esteem even, for example, while telling them off. It is sometimes a delicate line to tread, but a useful one.

Classroom managment

Comparing one class unfavourably with another. The intentions in doing this may be to encourage a competitive spirit. Few children, however, feel confident enough for this and a more common response is to give up. One class, for example, were praised and encouraged at singing while they were in reception. After the summer holidays when they returned as Year 1, however, they were suddenly not the best any more. In order to encourage the reception class, the teachers now praised the new pupils, saying that Year 1 should sing up as well as them. Some children in Year 1 were confused and angry. They were singing just the same as they had done before the holidays, but suddenly it was no longer good enough. What were they supposed to do in order to gain praise since they could not become reception children again? Faced with this impossible task, some children gave up and stopped trying to sing.

Criticism needs to be constructive and specific. 'Not good enough' and similar comments are frequently too general and imprecise to be of much assistance. Rather than being vaguely aware something is wrong, it is up to the teacher to analyse what is required for improvement and how this can be achieved. Comparing a class with their own best can be more helpful. For example, 'Last week you were singing just a little better because you were all opening your mouths beautifully. Open your mouths now and let the sound out . . . Yes, wonderful!'

Assuming a child, or children are not trying hard. There may be many reasons why a child produces poor work. He or she may be tired, upset, anxious, excited, ill, or may have undiagnosed literacy difficulties. As a criticism, 'not trying hard' is rarely specific enough to help children refocus. It can be more helpful to ask if they need help or to suggest they calm down, sit quietly on their own to do the work, keep bringing their thoughts back to the task when they stray, or do whatever else is necessary to focus well.

It may also be the case that some pupils whose behaviour is considered poor may at times be trying very hard. Indeed they may be trying harder than other members of the class who are never told off. It is, therefore, not a question of not trying hard but of lacking the skills to behave as requested or of having very powerful urges to act differently that have to be overcome. One dyslexic boy was clear about this and was very dispirited that even when he was trying his very hardest the teachers did not notice since, compared to other class members, his behaviour left much to be desired. To be told off for not trying when you are, in fact, trying extremely hard can be very demotivating: just what is the point of trying if no one even notices?

Punishing the whole class or a group for the misbehaviour of a few members. This is easy to do, especially if you are angry or unsure as to who exactly is responsible for the misbehaviour: for example, if something elicit is going on when your back is turned and, although you have your suspicions, you never quite catch the perpetrator in action; or if some class property has been damaged or has gone missing. Sometimes the hope is that some or the majority of the class will exert moral pressure on the miscreants so that they fall into line and stop misbehaving or own up to what has been done wrong. Unfortunately this is unlikely to work. Indeed, some pupils will relish the sense of power they can gain by inconveniencing the rest of the class or group. The pupils who are behaving well are likely to feel frustrated and powerless in the face of their peers' misbehaviour.

If a group seems to be noisy but you are not exactly sure who is talking, then splitting them up may help pinpoint who is responsible for the disturbance. If the class is unusually boisterous as a whole then this may be for a number of reasons: in response to an exciting event, a show or imminent trip, for example; as a result of wet playtimes inside; triggered by anxiety or reluctance to move on to another teacher next year, and so on. Sometimes it can help to comment on what is happening and why you think it is happening A couple of minutes spent in this way can help validate the children's feelings so that they can let go of them a little and settle down. More ideas for dealing with transitions are to be found in Chapter 3. A general restlessness may also, of course, indicate that the activity is not sufficiently engaging, is at an inappropriate level or has been poorly explained.

An approach which gives no room for the pupils to make amends or to improve their behaviour. Two boys in Year 5 were cleaning up after art. They were making a poor job of it and had left quite a lot of paint smeared on the tables. A teacher approached them and asked them if they had noticed the mess they had left behind, asking them to go back and finish the job. This gave the children the opportunity to put it right. It also gave the teacher the chance of praising them when they had finished the job completely. Another teacher tackled the same situation in a very different way, shouting at the two boys to stop immediately and go back to their seats. He then chose two other children to finish the job. This left the two boys feeling cross and humiliated. The teacher seemed to have assumed the boys had done the job badly on purpose. This might not have been the case. They might have intended going back to tackle the paint at the end or might not have even noticed it at that stage. The point is that the teacher made assumptions about the boys' behaviour and denied them any opportunity of putting it right.

Negative labelling. See the section 'Building confidence and self-esteem while 'telling off' in Chapter 5 (p. 120).

Punishments which are too harsh, are humiliating or give the child no hope of a way out. See the section 'Punishments' later in this chapter (p. 27).

Talking about a pupil in critical terms to a colleague or parent in front of other members of the class. If the aim is to bring about a change in behaviour, then public shaming is less effective than constructive criticism given in private. The former tends to result in anger, resentment and a loss of self-esteem. It can also help fix a child in a particular role as far as the class is concerned and this can subsequently make it more difficult for the pupil to change his or her behaviour.

A need to control rather than an expectation that you will remain in charge. An approach which perceives children as problems to be controlled tends to promote a confrontational style and is based on an assumption that children will definitely do wrong unless controlled. Many children become disaffected when on the receiving end of this approach. On the other hand, an expectation that you will remain in charge and an understanding that children are active participants in their own learning places the pupils on the same side as the teacher, sharing a common aim. This tends to foster a spirit of cooperation and goodwill. The first approach seeks to control the children, the second to remain in charge of the process in the classroom.

Rewards

Rewards are generally devised to improve motivation. However, some can be used in ways which can also demotivate. For example, a public system of commendation which singles out one or two pupils only for praise can be counter-productive, as in the following case.

One school had a system whereby children were awarded stars for good work. These were displayed on a wall chart. At the end of the week the child with most stars was awarded the special star. For the first term one Year 4 boy told his mum each week that he had failed to win the star. He was clearly disappointed that his efforts had not been good enough. During the second term he stopped mentioning the star. When his mother asked him about it he said that he, 'didn't care about it any more'. Since his efforts had not been rewarded, since he had been doing his best *without any guidance as to how he could possibly improve his performance* there was no point in trying any more. He did not know what else he could do, nor what he could do differently in order to win the star: he was in the position of being disempowered by the system. Rather than fail consistently, he had wisely chosen to opt out and cease to participate.

The problem with this kind of system is that most pupils fail each week. Even if the teacher is careful to rotate the awards so that everyone gets a turn, this would still only amount to a maximum of once or twice a year. This is a disincentive for many pupils who work hard since, although they may do an excellent piece of work, they might not get fitting acknowledgement if their personal 'quota' has already been used up. For most pupils this kind of commendation is neither immediate enough nor frequent enough to reward and encourage in a real way. There are many alternative systems.

As with any classroom management strategy, a useful starting point in considering a credit system is to ask the following questions:

- What is its aim?
- What are the likely consequences in the short and long term?
- Who is it for – you, the teacher; the school management; the inspectorate; parents, the children?
- Will it further the real education of the children, that is to say, will it build confidence and self-esteem; will it help them become independent and eager students with the skills to learn and understand?

Asking these questions of the star-chart system outlined earlier will soon expose the counter-productive nature of such a measure. Maybe one child will be encouraged for one week, maybe more if he or she wins repeatedly, but this is at the expense of huge demoralisation among the rest of the class. If the aim is to motivate, it clearly falls far short as a successful strategy.

Competition

The question of competition is an interesting one, some maintaining it is essential, others that it is damaging. Indeed, it is easy to fall into one camp or another on this issue, depending on personal experience. This in itself would perhaps indicate that it may be a more complex matter than it at first appears and some kind of a balance may be most effective.

As well as cooperating, human beings naturally vie with one another and to create an environment in which competing is considered 'wrong' is probably as unhelpful to many children as one which is highly competitive all the time. One boy in secondary school who was very good at sports always came second, even though when training his time often easily surpassed that of the winner. His parents could see him pulling up and dropping back in races as if he were deliberately avoiding first place. They spoke to his form teacher, explaining that he had been in a primary school where competition and winning were frowned upon, and asked her to talk to him, giving him permission to win. After she had talked to him about competing, making it clear that it was fine to try to win since someone had to, he began going for first and winning.

Rather than seeing competition or cooperation as opposing extremes, perhaps it is more helpful to think of ways in which all children can experience a sense of achievement. People who usually thrive on competition are those who are in with a chance of winning. Even if they do not succeed every time, they still have the possibility of doing so. There is something they can do about the fact they lose in order to improve their performance for next time: they can train harder, refine their skills, study more. In other words, *the possibility of success is close enough for the element of competition to be empowering: what you do can make a difference to the outcome.*

Most children, and especially those with low confidence and self-esteem, need to achieve regularly. They need to see progress, hear praise and feel the satisfaction of doing something well. If teachers can help pupils achieve regular successes in a range of ways, they will be building pupils' confidence as they learn. Without good enough confidence and self-esteem knowledge and skills are useless since they cannot be utilised. One dyslexic boy, for instance, had been taught spelling rules very thoroughly for three years. He knew the rules but was unable to apply them because he lacked the confidence to try things out and sometimes get things wrong. During a further four years of tuition aimed specifically at building confidence and changing his belief that he was no good at school he gradually became able to use what he knew. He later went on to get a good degree at university. Without the strategies aimed at raising his confidence this would have been less likely.

Even if not competing openly, children very often compare themselves with others, in many cases unfavourably. If classmates are on a different book in a reading scheme, for example, they consider they are no good at reading; if another pupil writes more, they think they cannot write well, and so on. In his book, *Britain on the Couch* (1998), clinical psychologist Oliver James is concerned that comparison and testing have an adverse effect on the confidence of children, particularly once they have reached the age of seven, eight or nine. He writes, 'Children who do badly do more social comparing than those succeeding, because they are searching for clues as to where they are going wrong and because they feel uncertain' (p. 118). It is not only children with literacy or learning difficulties who seem to suffer from comparison. For instance, a boy in reception was on the verge of giving up trying to read because his friend, who seemed on an intellectual level with him in other areas, could already read fluently. A study conducted in 1984 found that self-esteem was lowest among pupils in schools with higher ability pupils. An example of this is a six-year-old boy in a private school who thought his reading was poor, even though he could read quite fluently, because other children in the class were reading more advanced books.

Another point to consider is the fact that not winning, competing for a job and failing, not always being the best are, realistically, experiences awaiting most if not all of us at some time or other in life and maybe even frequently. In order to flourish, therefore, children may also need help in managing a degree of failure without losing confidence and self-esteem. Strategies which can contribute to this include:

- creating an ethos in which progress, effort and the ability to lose graciously are valued as achievements, as well as success;
- helping children develop their ability to assess their own effort and performance with tolerance so that if they have done well, they are aware of this even if they have not come first, and if they have not done well for some reason they are aware of what went wrong;
- an atmosphere in which each is valued for his or her unique contribution to the group rather than for measurable abilities.

It certainly seems to be true that it is less a case of what you know and more one of *how you feel about what you know*. Self-deprecating comparison is difficult to contend with other than by creating an ethos in which effort of all kinds is valued, difference is celebrated and achievements, however small and in whatever field, are lauded. It is also helpful if children are sometimes able to work on different pieces of work so that direct comparison is less likely. Collaborative work in which everyone's unique contribution is recognised can play a part in creating an ethos in which personal endeavour is valued.

Some additional points to consider regarding credit systems are:

- Children whose strengths are in areas less valued in the school system (using Gardner's model outlined in the next chapter this would be kinaesthetic, musical, spatial, inter-personal and intrapersonal) and other children with specific or other learning difficulties would never succeed in a straightforward contest involving literacy and numeracy skills. They would very easily become demoralised and disaffected.
- What kind of credit systems allow children to compete against their own personal best?

- If teams are contending are they evenly matched so that each team can win sometimes and can do something to improve its performance when it does not?

Other rewards

Children often appreciate the teacher bestowing a tangible acknowledgement of their good work or behaviour. This is true as long as they respect the teacher and the basis for bestowing rewards seems fair. There are a range of rewards employed, often on a whole-school basis, including praise, stickers, certificates, letters home, allowing the children choice and 'privilege time' outlined below. It can be fruitful devising a system of class rewards, based on school policies, with the children. This might involve them ranking in order of importance rewards you suggest and they may add some of their own. The more valuable the rewards are for the children, the more motivated they will be to earn them.

A system adopted by Susan House, the teacher writing at the beginning of Chapter 5, works as follows. Each child makes his or her own commendation book. This is a zigzag book using A3 paper. He or she then rules horizontal lines to make three columns each page, one for the date, one for the reason for the commendation and one for the teacher's signature. When the child has completed some good work the teacher draws a star on it when marking. The pupil then writes in the date and the reason, spelling it correctly, and asks the teacher to sign it. Commendations are given for any activity, including PE, art, cooking, or for good or cooperative behaviour. When a child has collected 15 commendations he or she is given a sticker by the teacher. For older pupils this could be replaced by something else, for example, a standard letter of commendation sent home. The books are stored standing in three tubs indexed alphabetically for easy retrieval.

This system allows privacy which can encourage children to concentrate on personal progress and on improving their own work rather than on comparing themselves with others. It requires minimal teacher input since the children take responsibility for recording commendations. The children also practise certain skills implementing the system.

Commendations for work are complemented by a competitive system of points awarded for a variety of activities, for example, sitting beautifully, working cooperatively, answering questions or following the class code. The class is divided into 5 or 6 groups. A running score of points is kept on the board each week. Members of the winning team can choose the game played in the last ten minutes on a Friday afternoon. This introduces an element of group competition. Consequently, the teacher keeps a check that teams win more or less equally, helping those with difficulties working together to learn skills which will enable them to win.

Choice

Some teachers find that rewarding children with a choice of activity is the most effective way of maintaining their motivation and avoiding disaffection. Choice can help children take responsibility and exercise their independence. The children enjoy this and the teacher ensures that all the activities promote the individuals' overall education. It is perhaps worth remembering that the most vulnerable children can find too free a choice frightening: they lack the confidence to take the responsibility of choosing and find it difficult to initiate a task. They need the structure of being told what to do. A boy in a reception class illustrated this very clearly. While the other children were purposefully engaged in their chosen activity he could settle at nothing. Instead he played with something for a few seconds or sat down to do a drawing and then wandered off to another child. Here he watched briefly before grabbing the child's toy, brush or pencil: he lacked the confidence to enjoy something by himself and lacked the skills to ask to join in with anyone else.

When dealing with children with very low self-esteem choice is often best introduced very gradually. To begin with, for example, rather than choosing the activity itself they could be given the choice of using your 'special' felt tips or 'special' coloured pencils to do a drawing. In this way they can gently build the confidence needed to commit themselves to one thing or the other without the fear of choosing the 'wrong' one.

Jenny Mosley (1994) proposes the idea of 'privilege time' which takes place for half an hour a week. Children decide which privileges they would like to try to earn through good work and behaviour. This allows the children choice and involves them in working for a meaningful reward.

Praise

Young children tend to thrive on praise and, as long as a good enough relationship has been established, will usually wish to please. With children from the age of 8 or 9, however, it is best to be more discriminating in your use of praise. A bland 'good' given in order to encourage even if the work or effort is mediocre will simply not be believed by many older children. When giving praise:

- Be genuine and sensitive.
- Be specific. Tell the children what it is they have done well. For instance, 'Well done, M, you came in and sat straight down to work today. That was lovely' or, 'Your story was well balanced with a beginning, a middle and an end. Well done! I really enjoyed it.'
- Leave constructive criticism till later; some children may be able to hold onto the praise if criticism follows, but most will not; if children are helped to develop their own ability to assess their work, many will sense something needs to be changed, even if they are unsure what exactly is needed. This allows the teacher to make tentative suggestions, for example, 'One thing you could do would be to . . . You may have another idea.'
- Use praise early on to help create a positive atmosphere. This may involve reminding the class how well they worked the day before, or praising them for the way they entered the room or how they are sitting at the time. If there seems little to praise them for and only some children are sitting quietly it can be tempting to mention the name or names of those who are doing so. The aim is for others to copy their behaviour. This can be effective as long as you choose different children as models. If one or two children are always singled out as those who are 'good', this can be counter-productive. Another way is to say, 'I

can see one person sitting well,' smile at him or her. 'No, I can see two, three, four, lots of you. Well done!'
- Be aware that some older children may prefer praise to be given in private. A boy in Year 3 mentioned in Chapter 3 was very clear that he did not want to 'shine' in class and did not wish to be singled out for public praise. Indeed, to avoid this he stopped working. In talking to him, the teacher understood his wishes and agreed not to praise him publicly.

Encourage children to praise each other. This is more likely if they have been involved in creating the reward system and there is an ethos of supporting one another in the class. They may also suggest class members should be rewarded for work, behaviour, effort or acts of kindness.

Difficulties with work

Never finishing work. It is, as you can imagine, quite demoralising if you are consistently unable to finish your work in time. For example, a dyslexic boy in Year 6 never finished his maths work and had to stay in at break to do so. He was totally disaffected by this and the task seemed more and more impossible to him all the time. If a child is regularly not finishing work, then it is up to the teacher to question why this is so and set a different or shorter task, give extra help or in some other way enable the pupil to finish. Sometimes children can or want to finish things off at home. This can be useful if it is on a voluntary basis or is used occasionally. If, however, it becomes a regular expectation it can contribute to a pupil's demotivation and suggests the tasks should be altered to meet the individual's needs.

Any demand which is inappropriate for the child's age or ability and which he or she is most likely to fail. As noted earlier, fairly confident pupils with good enough self-esteem can, with support perhaps, weather a little failure here and there since this is a natural part of life. For other children, however, it can simply entrench their sense of poor self-esteem and confirm their antagonism towards schooling. Moreover, Oliver James (1998) cites research which indicates that children tend to become less resilient towards failure as they go up through primary school. He sums up by saying, 'From ages seven to nine, self-esteem, self-confidence and optimism decrease at school' (p. 118). Frequent testing can be unfortunate in this respect since it can sometimes confirm children's perception of themselves as failures both by the result and by the experience of not being able to do or complete test tasks. Indeed, James (1998) also quotes experimental studies by Diener (1978) which show that when children were given low scores in tests, *even if they had actually performed well,* they began to show signs of learned helplessness, acting as if their actions could not make a difference.

Target-setting needs also to be applied with sensitivity so that targets are always realistic and achievable. The aim is that they are used to build confidence through gradual success rather than undermine it through failure. Some children are unable to try harder either because they lack the relevant skills and/or sufficient confidence. If a demand is inappropriate, whether it concerns behaviour or work, giving up before you start is sometimes easier and less painful since you cannot fail if you do not even try.

Homework. Schools will have their own homework policy. Within this framework, there may be some opportunity for flexibility. It is worth thinking seriously about the aims of the homework and asking yourself some questions.

- How will this contribute to the children's education?
- Do the children understand why they have homework and what it is for?
- Do they have any say over what they are to do and how they are to do it?
- Is this an interesting task? Is it likely to inspire the children to want to learn more? Will it motivate or add to their disaffection with school?
- Will it help pupils' understanding in any way?
- Do the children have all the skills needed to complete this task? For example, if it is a learning homework, do they have appropriate strategies for learning? Is it differentiated?
- Can the children fail at this task?
- Are the instructions clear and written down?
- Is it easy for parents and carers to get involved in the homework? Could the children still manage if there is no one to help?
- Is there sufficient structure for those who need it?
- Could you have done this homework when at the same age as your class? Would you have wanted to?

In addition, it is important to acknowledge homework appropriately when handed in. There are several aspects involved:

- It is usually necessary to help children remember to hand in homework. Without reminding, some might leave papers in folders for weeks. Pupils with SpLD often find it difficult to organise themselves and are likely to need help. Having a book for homework, or a folder if sheets are used, can ease organisation. Children who are poorly motivated may well not complete homework, forget or not bother to hand it in. If a child fails to complete homework on several occasions it is worth asking why: is the task too difficult, does it fail to interest him or her, is there insufficient support at home, and so on?
- Be flexible if work is handed in late. Although lateness will generally be unacceptable in secondary, it can be more fruitful in primary if teachers work with parents or carers to help children gradually learn how to take responsibility for remembering to do and hand in homework on time. For example, a girl in Year 5 with SpLD had spent considerable time and effort on a piece of work but had left it at home and handed it in one day late. The teacher said it looked interesting but refused to mark it even though he had not warned the girl of this consequence and it was the first time she had handed work in late. The effect on her was highly demotivating and she put much less effort into homework after this.
- Make it worth the children's while to try hard at homework by celebrating achievement and effort. Even when the children themselves or their parents mark homework a positive comment from the teacher is still needed.

If poorly thought out and inadequately structured, homework can contribute to a child's disaffection and dislike of school. It can become a battleground between parents and their children, a regular argument in which many parents feel obliged to cajole, encourage or coerce their children into completing tasks. This can be difficult, particularly if the instructions and aims are unclear.

Commenting on what is wrong, rather than what is right. This can apply to both work or behaviour. If a teacher tends to comment on a failing rather than first giving praise and only then noting, often privately, what needs to be improved, the effect can be demoralising. Obviously teachers need to help pupils improve their skills and sometimes their behaviour: the question is how this can be achieved as efficiently as possible. In his book *Positive Pupil Management and Motivation* (1999) written for teachers in secondary schools, the educational psychologist, Eddie McNamara suggests that an observer should note four positive teacher–pupil interactions for every one negative one.

Being aware of the emphasis implicit in feedback is also relevant as far as marking is concerned. When pupils do a piece of work what do you look for: what they can do and have done, or what they cannot do and have not done? Perhaps you look for both, but how do you report this information back to them? It is easy, when eager to do your job 'properly' and *teach*, sometimes to forget to acknowledge what has been done. Children need this acknowledgement, even if they have a lot to learn. Separating praise from points of instruction which come later can be very helpful. This is particularly relevant for pupils with specific learning difficulties who may themselves be deeply frustrated at their own inadequacy at expressing ideas in written form and whose confidence is very low.

It is not a question of not teaching, simply one of choosing the most appropriate time in which to do so. It can be helpful to remember that, by their very nature, children tend to learn if the environment is conducive to doing so, the information or skill has some relevance to them, they are interested in the topic or by the process of learning, and they are secure enough in order to concentrate.

Teacher assessment

There can be disadvantages to teachers being the sole assessors of the children's work and behaviour. One is that the teacher can be perceived as being unfair by the children, comparison is often easy, and the children are not encouraged to develop their own critical faculties. If, for example, they have worked hard and feel proud of their work and the teacher fails to give it due praise, the children might lose confidence in the piece of work and their own ability, or in the teacher who does not recognise their efforts. Conversely, if the teacher praises highly a piece of work the children considered poor, confidence in the teacher's opinion is likely to drop. If a child is reprimanded for something he or she did not do, it can lead to resentment towards the particular teacher and towards school as an unjust institution. *In all these cases, the child's experience is not validated.* Over time, this can lead to a loss of enthusiasm, learned helplessness, since effort and quality are not always recognised, or simply cynicism.

Another point to consider is the kind of marking teachers do. A report by Black and William (1998) which looked at 600 international studies involving over 10,000 pupils' claims that individuals achieve more when given feedback and encouragement rather than marks out of ten since many are demoralised by the latter. For children who do well, marks can be satisfying, confirming and rewarding, but comments could serve as well. For those who are trying hard yet achieving poorly marks may serve only to dispirit. For others who have missed work a low mark may give the message that catching up is too hard.

Another approach is intrinsic assessment which aims to help develop the children's ability to assess their effort, work and behaviour. For example, in some schools the children themselves are asked to choose one or two significant pieces of work per term to go in their own Special Work Book, a portfolio which follows them from class to class until they leave the school. The teacher's role is to be sensitive to the children's work, acknowledging with them the success of completing something special and helping others develop the confidence to recognise a piece of work which is particularly good.

Other schools ask the children to comment on their own work each week. They might keep a work journal in which they note their progress: what they enjoy, dislike, find easy or difficult, anything they are particularly pleased with and so on. Assessment would entail considering some simple questions, their number and complexity depending on the age of the pupils. For example:

- work I have done well this week, including any really special work;
- work I have enjoyed;
- any changes I could make in thinking, planning, doing;
- any changes I could make in working with others.

This need take only 5 or 10 minutes a week. With a class new to the idea of reflection on their work, it can be helpful if the teacher first leads a discussion on the questions and models how to assess work. During this, the teacher encourages children to be as specific and realistic as possible in their assessments and in their planning for change. The exercise can be presented as an exploration rather than a judgement: how could they learn most effectively? What do they need in order to understand? How could they work together better? It is useful if children agree to focus on a review of their *own* work rather than comparing themselves with others. Sometimes the pupils talk in pairs, summing up the week. Sometimes they write their ideas briefly in their journal.

The teacher reviews these periodically for several reasons. Firstly, in order to learn about the children's preferences which would help in future planning. Secondly, to spot any discrepancy between a child's perception of how he or she is working and the teacher's. Some children will probably be over-critical and will fail to recognise their strengths and the value of their work. Others might not be aware of unhelpful behaviour or of a technique which would help them. At the beginning in particular, some children will require considerable encouragement in assessing their work. Thirdly, the teacher's review will reveal those who need guidance in planning small achievable changes.

A combination of approaches can be employed in which the children are asked to put a comment on their work before showing the teacher. Assessment becomes a cooperative process in which teacher and pupil work together. Younger children could draw a smiley or sad face, or one with a straight mouth. Children with very low self-esteem may well need considerable external approval from the teacher and praise from classmates before they have the confidence to assess their own work as anything other than 'rubbish'. The children could also discuss their work with peers. (The use of writing partnerships is outlined in the following chapter.)

Intrinsic assessment encourages children to reflect on their work, how they go about it and their behaviour. Over time, it encourages independence and more realistic expectations. The children are placed in a position in which they do the work rather than sitting back to be assessed by the teacher. This avoids situations in which children consider a teacher as unfair or lose trust in a system they perceive as unjust. It also encourages them to compete against their personal best and to strengthen their internal sense of right and wrong.

5. Punishments

Punishments are usually a last resort and are best used sparingly. They should follow soon after the incidents for which they are given. They are most effective if the child in question and the rest of the class think they are fair and deserved. Children should never be deprived of a part of the statutory curriculum as punishment. Inappropriate punishments can contribute considerably to children's resentment and sense of demoralisation and cynicism. Disaffection is most likely when punishments are:

- given without proper warning, since this denies the child the power to chose to stop or change a behaviour in order to avoid the consequence of punishment;
- unduly harsh, since this seems unjust; a boy in Year 5 whose main interest in life was playing football was, for example, given 500 lines, 'I must not play football in the playground'. Such a punishment did little other than to feed his dislike of school since he was still desperate to play football at lunch times.
- applied inflexibly, for example, extenuating circumstances are not taken into consideration and children are not listened to;
- given to the whole class or the whole group for the misbehaviour of a few;
- meaningless activities since these are designed to waste the child's time in a very unconstructive way; for example, writing lines;
- given to a child who is trying hard to change behaviour even if improvement is slow; if he or she is punished as usual then it is likely to seem that all his or her efforts have been ignored;
- used to humiliate or shame pupils; a Year 6 boy, for example, was regularly sent to do his work in a reception class since it was considered that he was behaving like a baby and should therefore sit with the 'babies'.

It is, therefore, often quite a challenge to find punishments which are fitting and which maintain the child's sense of confidence and self-esteem while nevertheless making it clear that certain behaviour is unwanted, must cease and has undesirable consequences. Some questions it can be useful to ask when considering possible punishments are:

- What is the aim of this punishment? Is it, for example, simply to punish; is it meant as a deterrent for the individual concerned or as a deterrent for other members of the class; is it to remove the child from the class in order to calm down, stop distracting others, give you a break or get some work finished; is it to ensure the pupil understands the gravity of what he or she has done; or is it merely to reassert that you are in charge?
- Is this form of punishment likely to meet the aim?
- Was the child aware that this or some kind of punishment would follow his or her action? Does the child have an incentive to improve his or her behaviour and lessen the punishment? Or did he or she have that choice earlier?
- Is it too harsh?
- What may be the short- and long-term consequences? Is the punishment likely to add to disaffection? Will it help the child behave differently in the future?
- Is this punishment respectful of the child?

It is usually worth being aware of the range of sanctions available to you for minor, persistent or more serious incidents so as not to be caught off guard, meting out a punishment rashly and regretting it later. Certain forms of punishment may be common practice in your school or may have been agreed upon in a behaviour policy. Legally, punishments should be usual in the school, what a parent could expect, moderate, and given with good motives. As always when dealing with young people, it is helpful when considering sanctions to be sensitive and respectful, while maintaining boundaries kindly. If it concerns a child in a colleague's class it is often useful in more serious matters to consult the colleague in question. He or she knows the child and may have information which puts the incident in a different light. Here are some common punishments and comments.

A disapproving look can sometimes be enough to prevent poor behaviour going any further.

A quiet rebuke. This needs to be specific and respectful so that it neither humiliates nor embarrasses the child, particularly in front of others.

Keeping in at break or lunch time. If this is to be used it is important, for several reasons, that the child always has some time for play. Children need to run about in the fresh air after sitting still in a classroom for several hours. If they miss play then it is even less likely that they will be able to sit still, not talk, work hard, attend, and so on for the rest of the day. Such a punishment is, therefore, counter-productive since it invites more undesirable behaviour later on. For a child who may already dislike school or feel resentful about the system this is likely to embitter him or her all the more. One boy in Year 4 I worked with had his morning play taken away for the forseeable future. This gave him no hope, no incentive to improve. A way around this difficulty is to deprive pupils of playtime two minutes at a time, with a maximum of six minutes taken away per playtime. If a pupil has lost some play over a number of days in this way he or she could win it back by particularly helpful behaviour or good work. With this approach, punishments are not set in stone, *an improvement in behaviour is always acknowledged so that there is a built-in incentive to improve.*

Being moved in class. Often moving a child closer to you, away from certain classmates or to a different part of the room can both act as a sanction and prevent a situation deteriorating. Understandably, some children find it difficult not to talk if sitting next to a friend, or not to answer if a friend speaks to them. The need to please or stay friends with someone is frequently more pressing than the need to abide by a rule or please a teacher. After such an incident it can be helpful to have a word with both children, explaining that they will have to sit separately all the time if they continue to talk since this makes it difficult for others to work. They may ask for another chance. If this is the case, they will probably need to think through what they will do *differently* in order not to talk next time. If they sit together without doing this they are more likely to revert back to their usual behaviour. Sometimes it is helpful to ask the pupils themselves where they would work best.

Sending to another teacher to work in a different room. As we have seen, this can be used in a way which is intended to humiliate. It can also be applied more constructively. It can have the advantage of giving everyone a rest from each other and a time to calm down. It may also help a child finish a piece of work if he or she has got stuck in the role of demonstrating disruptive behaviour in class. If being sent to another room, children must have work with them which they can manage independently. One teacher greets any new arrivals sent from another class coldly and then ignores them apart from ensuring that they understand the work to be done and do not disrupt her class. At the end of their stay, however, she says that she hopes never to see them again under such circumstances but would like to see them over the next couple of days bringing her a particularly good piece of work. The children invariably produce this and bring it to her. She then praises them enthusiastically and warmly, thereby transforming a potentially negative inter-action into a positive one.

Sending to the deputy head or head. This depends on the degree of support given by management in the school on matters of discipline and procedures for this would be agreed at a school level. It is usually reserved for more serious incidents or persistent misbehaviour.

A word with a parent or carer or a letter home. Most parents and carers want frequent feedback about how their child is managing in class. Certainly they would prefer information about any difficulties before they become serious. Children rarely want their parents or carers involved so the threat of informing them can, in some cases, help them behave differently. There are examples in Chapters 3 and 5 of ways in which parents have been involved in helping their child improve his or her work and behaviour. This can be done indirectly by talking with parents in a positive way about their son or daughter so that they feel more relaxed and optimistic and change their expectations regarding his or her behaviour and work in school. It can also be achieved more directly by giving parents a specific role in monitoring or rewarding behaviour. This may be part of a written contract between the child, the parents and the teachers.

Finishing off work at home if time has been wasted in school. Some possible difficulties attached to this strategy have been discussed earlier and it is always worth wondering if the work was avoided because of a difficulty of some kind.

Depriving of a privilege. If this were a rare privilege and the pupil had no opportunity to make amends this could be a very harsh punishment indeed and could lead to resentment and demotivation. If it were a more regular privilege and the child could win it back through effort, it would be more constructive. Jenny Mosley's concept of 'privilege time' mentioned earlier this chapter can be useful in this context. Since privileges are earnt, some of them can also be forfeited as a result of undesirable behaviour, and won back through cooperative behaviour.

In cases when a change of behaviour is required in order to avoid punishment, then this is constructive only if the child has the understanding, skills, an awareness of the specific steps to take and adequate support to succeed in changing. More on this theme can be found in Chapter 5.

The experience is very different if you are on the receiving end of a classroom management style which is based on rules and punishments set by the teacher rather than on cooperation and a class code drawn up together. One consequence of the former is that, if frightened by the likelihood of punishment, children are more likely to lie, to cover up for friends or to blame others.

If punishments are harsh or arbitrary they tend to emphasise the teacher's need to punish and little else. If, however, they are rarely used, are given after appropriate warnings and follow as consequences to the children's actions, then they make more sense. For example, if the children make a mess, they tidy up, if they are unkind to someone, they find a way of being kind to or doing that person a good turn. This is very different from a punishment which is often unconnected to the misde-meanour and lacks the element of reparation. It is not just a question of the teacher versus the pupils since the children have the power to change their behaviour and avoid the punishment. This also helps children understand that behaviour which infringes the class code hurts or inconveniences others: it is logical and just that the perpetrators should be expected to make amends in some way.

Preventing the need for punishment

Obviously a more satisfying approach is to be able to prevent the need for punishment in the first place. It is usually the case that, when we, as teachers, are feeling good about ourselves and creative in our work the children in our class, on the whole, behave more as we would wish and receive fewer punishments. In other words, when we are feeling on top of the job and/or on top of the world, we can more often find creative and constructive ways to prevent or divert potentially troublesome behaviour.

Suggestions for preventing the need to give punishment occur throughout the book. Other and more specific ideas include:

- The classroom management strategies for creating a calm and purposeful environment cited earlier in this chapter.
- Stepping in early at the first sign of trouble.

- Helping pupils reflect on their behaviour, for example, by suggesting they go and tell a teacher they like how they are behaving at present. Usually the child does not want to go. If asked why not he or she invariably replies to the effect that he or she is behaving badly in some way or other.
- Thinking flexibly rather than intransigently when a potential area of conflict arises.
- Making expectations as clear and consistent as possible.
- Involving pupils in drawing up a class code.
- Giving clear warning of any consequences which might follow undesirable behaviour.
- Helping pupils become diverted by a new activity rather than getting stuck in trying to stop the troublesome behaviour.
- Providing interesting and meaningful activities.
- Providing work at a level suitable for all to achieve.

Since, as the professionals, we are in charge of the process in the classroom we are, in most cases, usually to some extent responsible for the fact that a child is being punished.

Thus, whenever we give a punishment it can be useful to consider two points:

(a) what we could do in future to prevent that kind of incident happening again;
(b) if it does what we could do differently to avoid the need to punish.

A common misunderstanding is that the idea of starting out with a firm manner at the beginning of the year or when teaching a new class means giving out lots of punishments. This is not the case, since it tends to set up an atmosphere of fear rather than of trust. Firmness refers to expectations, that is to say, that you are very clear in thinking through procedures and structures and clarify with the children the standards of behaviour required. This is best achieved by focusing on the desired behaviour rather than on what is not wanted. Going into a class and saying something along the lines of, 'Now, I don't want any trouble today!' may be seen as a challenge by some and may even suggest the idea of causing trouble to others who had not thought of it before.

This chapter has dealt with:

Establishing a calm and purposeful environment

- Entering the building and the classroom
- Ending a session and leaving the class
- Efficient personal organisation
- A seating plan
- A quick start
- Ongoing activites
- Purposeful to-ing and fro-ing
- Clear expectations: developing cooperation
- Sitting still
- Listening

Helping children develop relevant skills

Building confidence and self-esteem
Common causes of disaffection and some alternative strategies

- Classroom management
- Rewards
- Difficulties with work
- Teacher assessment

Punishments

- Preventing the need for punishment.

Chapter 2

Preserving motivation

Above all things we must take care that the child, who is not yet old enough to love his studies, does not come to hate them . . . His studies must be made an amusement: he must be questioned and praised and taught to rejoice when he has done well . . .

(Quintilian, *Institutio Oratoria*, AD 95)

As we have seen, most children come to school eager and able to learn if the conditions are favourable to do so. It is the teacher's task to preserve and nurture this natural motivation. There are many areas in which this can be done and these can be loosely grouped into the four headings below:

- helping children to feel successful as students;
- active participation: making real decisions about work, taking responsibility for learning;
- relevant, accessible activities leading out from the child's understanding to the larger world;
- fruitful relationships within the school.

The last point is addressed in Chapter 3. The first three points form the body of this section.

1. Helping children feel successful as students

Finding a way in

To understand how daunting it can be starting to learn to read and write it may be helpful for teachers to attempt to learn to read, or merely decode or write without understanding a different script, for example Arabic or Bengali. It is surprising how easy it can be to forget, confuse or not quite form correctly a new script. Since children are just beginning to write, it would be fair to try writing with the hand you do not usually use. This may give some useful insights into the kind of experience some of the children may be having. What can you do to help?

There is sometimes an emphasis on how to deliver a curriculum or on how to teach children, much less on *how to help them learn*. Yet, in a sense, that is what it is really all about. This change in perspective can sometimes lead to very different approaches. For example, if you are considering *how to teach spellings* to, say, a Year 1 or 2 class you are likely to adopt a very different technique than if you are thinking of how to help the 30 or so individuals in your class find the best way of *learning spellings*. In the former, you may group spellings into 'families' with similar letter combinations. You may teach the children the procedure of 'look, cover, write, check', and then send them home to learn a word family, with a note to parents explaining how to help. Some children will achieve this with no difficulty whatsoever since they have the learning strategies which make learning spellings easy. Some will work hard and, with parental help, manage to get most correct. For other children and their parents it will be an exercise in failure and frustration since they do not have appropriate learning strategies to succeed. On the other hand, if considering *how to help children learn spellings* you would proceed in a very different way, as outlined on p. 43.

Multiple Intelligences
The theory of Multiple Intelligences (MI) expounded by Harold Gardner (1983) suggests that there at least seven different ways in which humans experience the world. These are:

1. logical-mathematical intelligence, the intelligence of number and logical reasoning;
2. linguistic intelligence, the intelligence of words;
3. spatial intelligence, the intelligence of images and 3-D awareness;
4. bodily-kinaesthetic intelligence, the intelligence of the whole body;
5. musical intelligence, the intelligence of sound and rhythm;
6. interpersonal intelligence, the intelligence involving awareness of others and social understanding;
7. intrapersonal intelligence, the intelligence of self-awareness.

Whilst everyone has each intelligence, everyone does so in a unique blend of strengths and weaknesses. One adult with SpLD I taught, for example, had considerable difficulty with issues demanding linguistic intelligence but had a great talent with anything requiring bodily-kinaesthetic intelligence. He worked in the antique trade and simply by holding or feeling an item could tell if it was genuine or not; his reading was at a nine-year-old level, however, and his spelling at that of a seven-year-old. Another student may have strengths in the area of logical-mathematical, linguistic and musical intelligence and be lacking in development in the other areas, and so on.

MI theory has important implications regarding teaching. Our education system tends to develop, focus on and prize the linguistic and logical-mathematical intelligences above all. This can result in many children with strengths in other areas not really being touched by many aspects of the curriculum. They are the children who are easily demotivated by their experience of a school system which tends to neither recognise nor sufficiently develop their skills and interests and who either withdraw and fail to thrive as well as they might or who resort to disruptive behaviour. Harold Gardner (1991) and Tom Bentley (1998) outline the kinds of changes needed in our education system as a whole in order to engage all children and provide a more balanced education relevant to the twenty-first century. However, even working within the current system and within the constraints and limitations present, the individual teacher can nevertheless use MI theory to refine his or her skills and improve the experience of the children in the class in the following ways.

(a) By noticing, validating and helping develop children's different intelligences whenever possible. This can be difficult when emphasis is placed on basic literacy and numeracy skills and time for other activities seems limited. However, many of the techniques suggested throughout the book will provide some opportunity for children to use, develop and recognise their skills in a wider range of intelligences. For example, small group work and many of the activities in the following chapter give the opportunity for the acknowledgement and development of inter- and intrapersonal intelligence. So, too, can activities which enable children to develop links with the local community. Children being responsible for classroom displays, setting out exhibitions and the layout of a class book or magazine, as well as the more obvious areas of clay work, PE, drama and dance, can validate spatial and bodily-kinaesthetic intelligence. Setting multiplication tables to a tune or a rhythm could engage children with good musical intelligence, and so on.

Simply recognising a child's strengths and particular blend of intelligences, praising and encouraging whenever possible and devising opportunities for them to be used in activities can help children feel accepted and successful, even if they are weakest in the areas of linguistic and logical-mathematical intelligence.

(b) By using a variety of approaches in order to engage all children. Gardner talks of five entry points which are the ways in to activating the seven kinds of intelligence. These are:
   1. the narrational – telling and explaining the story within a topic;
   2. the logical quantative approach – using numbers or logical, deductive reasoning to understand new concepts;
   3. the foundational or philosopical approach – asking fundamental questions relating to a topic;
   4. the aesthetic approach – using and valuing sensory experiences connected to a topic;
   5. the experiential approach – understanding concepts by doing things.

Since the teacher will also have his or her own blend of intelligences and will, therefore, be attracted to particular entry points, ensuring a balance of approaches requires thought and planning. Without a balance some children are likely to lose interest and may resort to disruptive behaviour.

Neuro-linguistic Programming (NLP)

A theory at the basis of Neuro-linguistic Programming and explained by Bandler and Grinder (1979) suggests that people have different ways of operating when thinking, these differences corresponding to the three principal senses of vision, hearing and feeling (kinaesthetics). In other words, people think in one of three main representational systems. Internally, some will generate visual images, some will have physical sensations and some will have an internal dialogue or hear sounds. This theory can be seen to correspond loosely to the idea of multiple intelligences and different entry points as put forward by Gardner. It is also useful to consider, however, since it can readily be applied in the classroom.

One of the ways of assessing a person's representational system is by noticing the kinds of predicates (verbs, adverbs and adjectives) that she or he uses to describe personal experience.

- A visual representational system will tend to use words such as, 'look, see, show, focus, perspective, view': 'I can see what you mean'; 'Let's focus on this'; 'How would you view the problem?'; 'It looks good to me'.
- A kinaesthetic representational system would favour, 'grasp, handle, feel, smooth, grips, rough'; 'I feel that's very important'; 'I get the sense you're not with me'; 'I get the feeling it's pretty tough at the moment'.
- An auditory representational system might choose: 'sound, ring, resonate, hear'; 'It sounds good to me'; 'It doesn't quite ring true'; 'I can hear what you're trying to say, but . . .'

As with an awareness of Multiple Intelligences, an understanding that people think and, therefore, learn in different ways is crucial since it touches upon the heart of a teacher's task: namely, finding a way in to involving each child in exploring and developing.

If a child knows which is his or her strongest representational system he or she can employ this in learning. If the child is unaware, he or she may unwittingly employ the least successful strategy and fail, or manage but with unnecessary difficulty. An example will clarify my point. Although I found much school work relatively easy, there was one aspect in which I consistently failed: learning 'by heart'. This was because, misunderstanding the task, I employed my weakest representational system for the job. Since we would be called upon to recite a poem learnt 'by heart', I believed I had to learn it by saying it aloud. Consequently, I would read a line or two and then close my eyes, whilst repeating it over and over, *listening* to the words. Using this technique I managed *not* to learn considerable amounts of poetry, including poems I really loved and wanted to know! Had I *looked* at the poems, thereby using my primary representational system, and had I linked the words to images in my head, I would have had greater success. I might also have written the poem out using my second system (kinaesthetic), perceiving the words as I did so. The fact was that my teachers did not understand the importance of presenting a range of learning strategies and left to chance the kind of strategy children adopted.

When learning foreign languages, however, I soon realised I could remember little or nothing unless I saw it written down. I would write new words in a book and read them over from time to time. Consequently, I learnt to speak foreign languages first and foremost by reading (visual), secondly by writing new words down (kinaesthetic), and only thirdly by listening and speaking (auditory). Helping children, therefore, to understand their own process and individualise their method of learning can be of great value. Fitting the right kind of learning technique to the task is also helpful, as is using a number of different strategies or stages.

Children who have a kinaesthetic primary representational system often find greater difficulty with literacy skills than those with either an auditory or a visual one. This is simply because it is easier to recognise and remember words by sound or visual image than by how they feel. Imagine, for example, trying to spell 'cough' or 'difficult', or even 'one' or 'top', if you are relying on how they feel without integrating information about how they look or sound! Reading would also seem extremely difficult and confusing.

If children are aware of their major representational system and, therefore, of how they tend to set about a task, they can be taught to employ other methods to compensate if necessary. They can be encouraged to strengthen their weaker systems, whilst using their major one as appropriately as possible. Making a link between one system and a stronger one can be extremely helpful.

Children with a highly developed kinaesthetic representational system may well find difficulties in other aspects of school life, since they may be more attracted to *moving,* and *doing* rather than sitting still and listening, speaking, writing, looking or reading. Since many teachers will have managed the academic demands of school life with some ease there is likely to be a high percentage of teachers with a primary visual or auditory representational system. Consequently, children with the kinaesthetic as their major system may feel less connection with a greater number of teachers than their peers. In some cases this disaffection and lack of contact in school may lead to disruptive behaviour.

Curriculum demands may leave little time for considering and teaching skills concerned with the *process* of learning. However, consideration of this process can help children learn more independently and achieve more. This is explored in more detail later this chapter.

'Joy in learning'

'Joy in learning' is a key point put forward by W. Edwards Deming (1994) as a way of improving education. The essence of it is that students learn best when they are enjoying themselves. Certainly it is interesting to note that for some years now sections of the business world have understood that people work much better when they are happy in their job and enjoy their work. In some industries where it is possible to measure performance effectively it has been found that productivity rises when people enjoy what they are doing, feel supported, are given responsibility for their work and have an opportunity for exercising creativity. It is, therefore, reasonable to assume that children, and indeed teachers, will work better and achieve more if they enjoy their work and experience conditions which foster independence and creativity.

This leads to the question of how a teacher can structure activities so that children *enjoy* learning. In other words, what do children need in order to enjoy their time in school? I would suggest:

- the opportunity to feel successful;
- the opportunity to be creative;
- the opportunity to play, explore and try things out without fear of making mistakes;

- good enough relationships with teachers and peers;
- subject matter and/or a process which engages them.

Enabling learning

How young children learn
It is useful to be aware of the things that might take place in schools which can hinder children's learning. A retired nursery head teacher, Liz Murphy, gave the following suggestions.

- *Focusing on the 'end product' rather than the process.* Offering children opportunities to be creative, helping them to use the right tools, and giving them a range of choices, will have more relevance to their learning than producing a designed end product.
- *Sitting down too much.* Young children are developing their bodies as well as their minds and they need lots of opportunity for active and creative play. Sitting at their tables for long periods, writing, drawing or colouring in uses only a small part of their learning potential and quickly leads to boredom and a later unwillingness to concentrate.
- *Learning new concepts before they are ready.* Children build up their learning from previous experience. They need opportunities to play and experiment so that they 'understand' before more formal learning takes place. The best classrooms offer a full range of activities, including sand, water and home corner and the staff know the children well so that they can intervene as appropriate.
- *An over-directed curriculum.* Children learn best when they are self-motivated. They will practise a skill until they have mastered it, for the pleasure of success. It is important to gear the curriculum to the children's interests and to be prepared to make changes to existing plans. Most learning goals can be introduced through any subject or medium and the successful teacher is responsive and adaptable.
- *Unnecessary rules.* Children are very aware of fairness and will usually abide by a rule if they see it to be relevant. They need clear, firm boundaries which they understand. Often rules can get in the way of learning and can be a waste of time if they do not reflect the needs of the school community. Children are also very good at making their own rules, particularly in self-initiated games, when they want to sustain their imaginative play with a group of friends (Bruce 1987).
- *Thinking that the most important activities are teacher led.* Some of the most exciting and creative learning is done when the children have chosen their own activities. For instance, there is much more valuable learning from playing with blocks where they can talk, discuss, negotiate, compare and share with one another, than sitting at a table counting and sorting. Children get enormous pleasure and satisfaction from their early writing, like pretend shopping lists or filling in forms, which takes place in real situations. They are learning actively, through play and this can be developed and extended.
- *The belief that real learning only takes place indoors.* Children need to be outside in a well organised space that helps to develop their gross motor development. They need the experience of a safe, challenging play area that gives them the freedom

to move and is respected as an important part of the learning environment. *All* learning can take place outdoors. Some learning can *only* take place outdoors.

• *No time to respond to the emotional needs of the children.* Many children arrive with emotional luggage that needs to be acknowledged. Offering time to engage in creative and imaginative activities, or large physical play outdoors, can help them to express themselves and settle into the day. The classroom needs to be set out to accommodate this and encourage free choice. There also needs to be a welcoming, comfortable area for looking at books and quiet play.

Authors of *Design for a Life* (1999), Patrick Benson and Paul Martin emphasise the importance of play and of children being active in their own learning. They write:

The belief that play has a serious purpose – that of acquiring skills and experience needed in adulthood – is an old one. Modern science supports this belief.

One of the most important messages to emerge from biological research is that individuals are active agents in their own development – seeking out and acquiring experiences, sensations and skills that they will need later in life . . .

Play is an effective mechanism for facilitating innovation and creativity . . .

(Quoted in the *Guardian*, 31 August 1999)

Starting off reading and writing
Some recent research indicates that synthetic phonics may be a more effective tool than analytic phonics. Whichever system is used, however, major questions facing the teacher are:

• how to put it into context: what are the children learning phonics for?;
• how to help the children enjoy the process of learning;
• how to make it as easy for them as possible, in other words, how to activate the individual learning strategies of each child;
• how to enable children to use their new phonic knowledge successfully in reading and writing.

Some children learn to speak early on and, by eighteen months, have quite an extensive vocabulary; others do not reach the same level of verbal sophistication until around three or later. This is quite within the broad band of 'normal' speech development. There is also a similarly wide range of time involved in the normal development of literacy skills and it is worth remembering that the optimum age for some children to learn these skills will be at least seven years. In the classroom, this natural variation is compounded by other issues: for example, age differences in a year group; the educational levels of and the encouragement given by parents and carers; the child's preschool experience.

Without the desire or need to learn progress can be hindered. Most children are inherently interested in learning as long as the conditions are sufficiently enticing and they can succeed. Some lack confidence. One Bengali girl I taught had been in school for nine months and had apparently made little progress in her spoken English. She did not speak in English in class and rarely communicated with a teacher, then doing so only by using her friend as interpreter. This continued despite much encouragement until the class started going to a games field by coach and her friend happened to be absent. That day the girl explained very clearly in English that she did not want to go on the coach because she got travel sick. Up till this time she had never spoken in English not because she could not but *because she had no need to do so*. As in all learning, the children must desire to participate and see the need to do so either because they want to please parents or the teacher, they want to find out or acquire something for themselves, they enjoy the process, and so on. It is the teacher's task to maintain and, where necessary, create that desire or need to explore.

Ways of helping children learn letter shapes and sound and number are included in 'Learning spellings' in the section 'Helping children find the best learning strategy' later in this chapter (p. 43).

Handwriting

Different developmental stages will also affect how children learn to form letters. Some children, for example, have tremendous difficulty holding a pencil. Some are very tense, grabbing the pencil so hard their knuckles are white. This tension makes writing very difficult and is tiring. Others have difficulty controlling the pencil, and so on. If a teacher uses strategies which will enable even these children to succeed, then all children will probably benefit. A helpful way for many children is to start making big shapes in the air, tracing around large textured letters or painting bold patterns. Many children enjoy 'painting' letters and shapes on outside walls using water and a thick brush. Games can be useful too, children moving cars or animals around a track or paths that are in the shape of letters. The aim is to free children to create shapes found in writing and to become familiar with the movement needed to form letters without the fear of making mistakes.

Some awkwardness and tension can be avoided if children imagine the movement is flowing from the movement centre used in martial arts, the 'dan tien' or 'hara', in the centre of their bodies three or four finger widths below their navel, rather than from their wrists or fingers. It can be particularly effective to trace letters very slowly in the air imagining a string of feeling, sound, light or colour coming from the movement centre, up the body, down the arm and flowing out through the fingers.

Self-perception

Ensuring that children who are not yet ready to develop literacy skills nevertheless succeed in school is important for many reasons. In one nursery I observed a four-year-old consistently failing at a reading exercise. The exercise itself was poorly set up and age-inappropriate, consisting of whole words on cards without pictures. The task was to insert the correct word in the gap to complete the sentence, for example, The —— jumps over the gate. The teacher read the sentence aloud. There were three word cards for the child to choose from, including the correct one, 'dog'. Neither the task nor the words in the sentence held any meaning for the boy who was rapidly learning nothing other than he could not do this sort of thing. Since some children in the group could insert the correct word, the teachers expected the boy to be able to do so too. He was definitely perceived by others to be failing and, judging from his body posture, seemed confused, angry and frightened by this.

Once you *believe* something is too difficult for you, especially when others appear to succeed, your ability to understand usually plummets because of the feelings attached to failure. To avoid such feelings many children will develop alternative behaviour strategies, looking away, shuffling on the chair, crying, getting up and wandering off, creating a diversion through using humour or unwanted behaviour, for example, hitting a neighbour or chatting.

Any reception class may well have one or more children in it who can already read fluently on entering school, others who can recognise a few words, some who will not read fluently until they are eight or nine and others with a learning difficulty of some kind. It is important that those who find literacy difficult, perhaps because they are not yet at the appropriate developmental stage, are not alienated by repeated early failure. This has several implications:

- the aim and nature of tasks must be carefully thought out and altered as necessary to ensure success most of the time;
- expectations are generally best tailored to fit each child, progress being measured in the context of the child's own development;
- it is usually most effective for testing and test results to be handled with sensitivity. Even if the teacher plays down the significance of testing at Key Stage 1 some children may well pick up that they are doing something which is considered to reflect their ability. For those 'below the national average' and their parents this may be unhelpful. By the time of Key Stage 2 tests children are already more entrenched in their perception of themselves as successful or unsuccessful students.

Specific learning difficulties (SpLD)

If the natural time range for picking up literacy skills is so broad, how then can a teacher be alerted to the fact that a child may have specific literacy difficulties? How can a teacher distinguish between later development and a specific learning difficulty? This is an important question since some children are not diagnosed as having SpLD even by the time they are well into secondary school. Early recognition is extremely helpful and not doing so can be very damaging. One ten-year-old boy I taught with severe visual and auditory difficulties had not been diagnosed as having SpLD by his school even though his mother had been telling his teachers there was a problem since he was seven. She had noticed how he changed emotionally whenever he had to do reading or writing. He had been a happy, placid boy but had developed frequent fits of crying and temper. See the Appendices (A) for a definition of SpLD (Dyslexia, Dyspraxia, Specific Language Impairment and Attention Deficit/ Hyperactivity Disorder) and guidelines for recognising them.

The experience of failing in school, of feeling stupid, of doubting themselves and of fearing being found out usually compounds the initial literacy difficulties experienced by children with SpLD and further hinders progress. As one girl wrote:

Dyslexia

I enter the world like everyone else
in my clear box.
As time passes
people start to emerge
and indulge in life's pleasures.
I can see the light shining above
like a door of hope,
yet here I am tied
down by invisible cords.
Stupidity imprints itself
in my brain
as I strain . . .
The box closes itself upon me,
smothering,

and tears stain the crystal bottom
of the tomb.
The others crowding:
Stupid! Stupid!
Dumbo! Thicko!
Slow-
coach!
Am I the only one?
I cry for help.
Sleep my only rest
from torment.
But even here the echoes screech:
Stupid! Stupid!
Dumbo! Thicko!
Slow-coach!

Mikaela Davies, aged 10

The extent to which young people and adults are able to hide and divert attention away from some learning difficulties is impressive. For example, one man in his fifties with dyslexia had managed to hide from his own daughter, then an adult, that he had a very low reading age and could write little beyond his name! Suffice it to say here that, if a child is consistently misbehaving and/or produces written work which is disappointing considering oral performance, one avenue to investigate thoroughly is that of a possible specific learning difficulty. This is the case *even if the common mythology in the school is that he or she is simply disruptive or lazy* and more experienced teachers tell you the same. One 14-year-old girl in a maths class I worked in was considered just that. Observing her avoidance strategies and what she could and could not do it became clear that she was dyslexic. This was found in fact to be the case and she was given help.

Children learning English as an additional language may also be dyslexic and/or dyspraxic. This is useful to remember since poor literacy skills may be attributed to the fact the child is not working in his or her mother tongue. This may not be so. For example, a 12-year-old girl orally fluent in Arabic and English had great difficulty with written English due to dyslexia. Since she was a second language learner however, it was easy to assume her difficulty in producing written work was due to using English rather than because of a SpLD. If a child is exhibiting disruptive behaviour, is withdrawn or does not appear to be making the kind of progress you might expect and is a second language learner, it is worth checking for SpLD.

Unfortunately, misdiagnoses concerning children with SpLD are not uncommon and it is not surprising why. Many teachers are not made sufficiently aware of the pointers which may indicate SpLD, nor of what these difficulties really mean for the child in the classroom. Add to this the smokescreen of withdrawn or disruptive, maybe clowning behaviour or rudeness and the fact that children who disrupt lessons are invariably behind with work. It is a question of the chicken and the egg: which came first, the disruptive behaviour, or the difficulty with work. Obviously not all disruptive behaviour is due to a learning difficulty, it is, however, always worth carefully checking this out as a possible cause or a contributing factor.

Helping children find the best learning strategy

Learning spellings

For a number of children and their parents or carers, learning spellings at home becomes a time-consuming weekly nightmare which can undermine confidence and motivation while producing dubious results. This is often because insufficient time is spent in class helping the children develop effective learning strategies they can use at home. Parents are also usually unaware of the range of ways spellings can be learnt. Below is a selection of techniques which acknowledge the different representational systems children might use in learning.

David Perkins in *Outsmarting IQ* (1995) has developed a theory of 'realms', that is to say, any activity or topic people can come to know their way around. A realm is made up of three groups of elements: actions, beliefs and concepts. He proposes that the realm of memorising is made up of:

An action system, including:

- rehearsing;
- organising ideas into categories;
- finding links to something you already know;
- inventing visual associations;
- testing yourself, and concentrating on what you miss.

A belief system including such beliefs as:

- rehearsal aids memory;
- my memory is good or not so good;
- when I organise something for myself, that helps me remember it;
- visual associations help me remember things.

A conceptual system, including the concepts of:

- memory;
- rehearsal;
- association;
- image;
- organisation;
- forgetting.

The process of 'look, cover, write, check' includes some of the stages involved in an action system, but not all. A system which involves all stages and also takes into account the different representational systems children may have as strengths is likely to make memorising both easier and more effective. In essence, the teacher is endeavouring to help children *find their own way around* a system which, in this instance, is spelling but may also be times tables, facts, scientific terms, and so on. Encouraging children to talk about why and how they learn and experimenting a little to see which strategies work best for them can save a lot of time and effort and can be more fruitful in the long run. For example, ask children to consider why and how they have learnt a variety of things, maybe riding a bike, swimming, a poem, spellings, tables, and so on. Sharing experiences is likely to highlight the following points:

- there are specific ways of going about learning different things;
- individuals also use different strategies;
- there is no 'right' way since it depends on what works best for them;
- they can choose and experiment to see if they are employing the most effective techniques for them for individual tasks.

This process can help children set about learning in a more conscious way, reflecting upon the effectiveness of their chosen technique. It also gives many the confidence to experiment and helps them take responsibility for and feel in charge of their own learning.

Once children can find their way around learning spelling, for example, it is no longer an alien, confusing topic but one which has order and makes sense, despite all the many exceptions there are, then it is possible to experiment with greater confidence, to guess and to play. It is also easier to concentrate and to remember. Similarly, once children feel at home at working with number they can begin to feel more in charge, more comfortable and can then direct more brain activity to the problem in hand. The aim is to help the children in your class make sense of the process of learning and to guide them towards finding the most effective method for them to use for any purpose.

(i) Rehearsal

Rehearsing includes practice of any kind. *Multisensory* techniques can aid learning for many. This can involve, for example, making words with magnetic letters, sounding out as the word is built. The children can also write letters in sand, or paint and decorate large letters with different textures (sand, lentils, rice, silk, velvet, etc.). These can then be used for children to learn the shape of the letters by running their fingers over the textured letters. They can also be used to form words. As literacy skills become more developed, rehearsal may include making up and taping songs of rhyming rules or of difficult letter combinations, or working out and performing a sketch in which children play different letters or groups of letters so that they have plenty of visual, kinaesthetic and auditory associations with spellings.

One effecive way of helping children rehearse spellings is to play games. These can obviously be adapted to fit the age and literacy skills of children. Some suggestions can be found in the Appendix C.

A selection of games can be kept in the classroom and used as short activities for children to choose when they have finished their work and at other times to help with spellings. If instructions are available, some parents and carers might also like to play them with their children at home.

(ii) Organising ideas into categories

Playing with magnetic and other letters can help children organise and categorise new material, that is to say, can enable them to begin to make sense for themselves of the connection between sound, symbol and meaning. Other forms of organisation include:

Word 'families'. Spellings are given in groups of words which share certain letter combinations. Children can then highlight the common letters in different colours or by underlining.

Rhymes and rules. These can be particularly helpful for some children, for example, *'magic 'e'' 'you can see (c) two s's with ary on the end'*, (necessary); *'i before e except after c'*, (piece, ceiling), and so on.

(iii) Finding links to something you already know

The process of playing about with letters, sounds and words can also help children make links with things they already know. Such associations make it possible not only to remember but also to feel at home and confident with new material since it becomes your 'own' by being linked to the familiar. One six-year-old girl who found it difficult to remember or relate to numbers, did so by making her own associations so that they seemed less alien and more accessible. She thought of number one as a skinny boy, nine was a pregnant woman, ten was Queen Victoria, and so on.

Another way of making links is to break words up in order to find familiar words within words, for example: to-get-her, Sun-day, or noting familiar letter combinations, 'ing', 'ed', 'ion', 'ai', 'ou', and so on.

(iv) Inventing visual associations

It can be particularly helpful to encourage children to perceive. Telling them to 'Look, cover, write, check' makes the assumption that when they look, children know how to perceive. Some will, but many will not unless strategies are pointed out to them. Some questions for children to ask themselves which might help perception are:

- Is the word long or short? How many letters?
- Are there any tall letters? How many and where are they?
- Are there any letters with tails? How many and where are they?
- Are there any groups of small letters together? If so, what are they?
- What is the overall shape of the word?
- What is the first letter sound?
- What is the last letter sound?
- How many syllables?
- Are there any familiar letter groupings, beginnings or endings, for example, 'ing' at the end or 're' at the beginning?
- Are there any words inside the word?

(v) Visualisation and imagination

This involves employing children's imagination and can be used initially when children are learning letter sounds. What do letters look like and remind them of? Children can draw the letters with their associations. How does this link into the letter sounds? It can be equally fruitful to strengthen children's ability to 'see' letters, letter combinations and words in their head. They look at their decorated letter or word and attempt to perceive it in detail. Then they close their eyes and try to see it in their imagination, on the inside of their eyelids, perhaps. Some children will find this very difficult, but if it is presented as a game or an exploration they will find it interesting to experiment. For example, they might imagine it as part of a picture, linked to an object or in a particular colour. Some children will be able to imagine the movement as a letter or a word is written 'in their heads', or 'see' it as part of a larger picture, or as part of their visual association. One girl with SpLD imagined and then wrote the word 'white' inside the open mouth of a great white shark. She was very interested in animals and this helped her recall the spelling since it was linked to something about which she was knowledgeable and felt confident.

(vi) Testing yourself, and concentrating on what you miss

It can sometimes be fruitful if the emphasis in learning is placed upon experimentation and the process of acquiring effective techniques for committing something to memory rather than upon test results. Children who learn spellings easily will do so anyway and those who find it difficult are less likely to become discouraged at an early stage. It can sometimes be helpful if children test themselves and then use this as a basis for perceiving what they do not yet know. In this way testing becomes part of the learning process rather than an exercise in getting a result. Another strategy which can sometimes be effective is for the children to hand in their papers on which they have written their spellings without names so that the teacher can get a view of how the different levels of spellers in the group are managing and what techniques he or she might need to employ in order to help those who are obviously experiencing difficulties.

It is common for children to spell words correctly in a test and then incorrectly in a story or other pieces of writing. This calls into question the effectiveness of regular testing alone as a means of encouraging children to incorporate correct spellings in written work. A strategy which can be useful is that of writing partnerships. When children have finished a first draft they share their work in groups of two or three. The aim is for children to give each other constructive criticism and help on such matters as spelling, punctuation, structure, language and specific ideas. In order to do this effectively, children will usually need a model, practice and guidelines. The teacher can model the process by leading discussions about pieces of work shown on an overhead projector. During this he or she can illustrate how to give constructive criticism and what to look out for. In their small groups, the children then work on an anonymous passage. Children will inevitably compare their work. Consequently, if this strategy is to build confidence in writing and help children express themselves more effectively, it is important that there is an atmosphere in which everyone's contribution is valued. The aim of the exercise is to help one another and to learn from each other. It is an opportunity to celebrate difference. Drawing up guidelines for working together can provide the forum for discussing this.

If the children are adequately prepared, this strategy can help them:

- develop their abilities to reflect on their own writing and that of others;
- practise talking about their work and the process of writing;
- sharpen their perception in checking for errors in punctuation and spelling;

- develop a sense of responsibility for and pride in their work;
- work independently from the teacher and collaboratively with peers;
- become more confident writers.

Learning tables
There is a range of activites which can help some children get to grips with learning tables. Some suggestions for games can be found in the Appendices. These could be used as homework activities, to help children experiencing difficulty with tables, during wet play or when main tasks have been completed. Practice might also include setting tables to music, perhaps a well known song tune, so the class could sing them together.

(i) Real uses
Practice in 'real' situations will help children not only learn tables, but also feel more confident in using them and, very often, see the point of them.

Cooking
If the children can be involved in cooking this can help them understand a practical use for multiplication. They could be given the ingredients for one portion and then have to work out what is needed for a group. The school cooks could come and give the class some examples of how they have to estimate portions using multiplication. Planning the food needed for a class party or school event could again furnish children with an experience of multiplying which would be more memorable and have more meaning than abstract sums on paper.

Shops
If there is a tuck shop in the school children could be involved in observing and helping work out estimates for buying and selling, projected profits, etc. Local shopkeepers could come to the school or the children visit shops nearby to learn about practical uses for multiplication. Working out what is the best bargain, large packets of cereal or small, packaged fruit or loose, and so on, can provide opportunities for using multiplication and division with a purpose.

A class or, indeed, the whole school might like to create its own supply of currency. This could be using play money, with banknotes added, or cardboard money made by the children. There could be many opportunities for practising various aspects of maths with this. For example, the children could 'buy' paper and 'rent' pencils, working out how much each table would have to pay to do so. Each group could also work out how much they would have to 'pay' the kitchens for lunch, and so on.

Interests
If the maths is 'translated' into a real situation which has meaning for children they are not only more likely to produce more work to a higher standard, they are also more likely to understand what it is all about. One Year 3 teacher was working on number bonds. She had previously asked the class to explore how many ways you could make 15, using just two numbers. When she did it a second time using

marbles, the amount and quality of work produced was far better. This was not attributable simply to the fact that the children were more familiar with the task since the process itself was also very different. On the second occasion, the children were fired with enthusiasm, set to work eagerly, remained more focused throughout and worked more quickly. The differences in both the process and the result were notable.

In this particular school, most of the summer term is the 'marble season' when children are allowed to play marbles, according to set rules, during breaktimes. Since it was June, the subject was very topical. The teacher brainstormed with the whole class the different kinds of marbles available. Working in pairs, children then chose two kinds of marbles and explored how many different ways they could make 15 using them.

Marbles themselves, or even the idea of marbles could be used to help children work out tables and understand the process. Anything reasonable that might capture the children's imagination or interest could be used.

Similarly, some tables could be practised using the children themselves, standing in groups of two's or three's, etc. If each child brought in a soft toy or made a cardboard model of an animal, for example, tables up to and including the five times could be practised in this way. In a spacious area, children could be asked to stand in groups of 2, 3, 4 or 5, depending on the table to be practised. A group at a time would move to a different section of the space as the table was recited. Each group could be counted to make up the new number. They could also hold up the number that they were in the table. In the three times table the first group of 3 would hold up number 3, the second a 6, and so on. In this way the children could see, count and feel the numbers in a very concrete way. The teacher could go on to set questions, for example, $5 \times 3 = ?$ and the children would have to move and work them out. This is particularly helpful for children whose primary representational system is kinaesthetic. It also encourages an understanding of what tables really are.

(ii) Individual learning strategies

It may also be helpful for the children to work to their strengths in setting about learning tables. If they can discuss how they best learn, explore their own strategies and reflect on the process they will usually be able to find very creative ways of assimilating new material.

Visual representational system

A girl in Year 4 had been asked to write out two tables a week in order to learn them. After doing so conscientiously for some months she still did not know her tables and was losing confidence in her ability at maths, thinking that she 'Couldn't do maths' because she did not know her tables when many of her classmates did. Talking to her about what she remembered as the most powerful impressions from holidays or from visiting new places, it seemed that her strongest representational system was visual, kinaesthetic being her weakest one. Consequently, writing tables out was a poor learning strategy for her unless linked to other systems.

She then decided to concentrate on one table a week and to write it out in an artistic way. She choose one colour to represent each table and wrote each out over the weeks in a different style, with various illustrations and visual prompts. For the three times table, for example, she chose green and presented it in two columns, the top three lines of each column in a cloud and the bottom three in a speech bubble. Presented in this way, the table made more sense to her, had a clear visual form, was divided into managable chunks and became possible in a way it had not been before: she had made it her own and could at last 'see' it. She stuck the completed table up in her room, referred to it frequently and was confident in using it within a week. Her general confidence in her maths increased markedly during the term.

There are many ways children could play with presenting the table in a visual form using paints or coloured pens. Some, for example, might like to take just one line of the table at a time, writing, drawing or painting it prominently, maybe with illustrations or within a picture. They then look at it and perceive the numbers before closing their eyes and trying to see the numbers on the back of their eyelids. If their auditory system was their next strongest they could also repeat the table as they looked at it, or listen to it on tape, as below.

Auditory representational system

Again, there are many possibilities for individual learning. Children could learn the tables 'by heart' by repetition. They could read one table a week onto tape and listen to that frequently during the week, looking at it or writing it out, depending on which system was stronger. They could read each table in a different kind of voice or accent so that the particular sound of that table made a greater impression on them. Similarly, they might like to set the table to music or say it with a particular rhythm, anything that would spark their imagination and unlock their learning potential.

Kinaesthetic representational system

Children who learn best by feeling or doing often experience the greatest difficulty in learning tables. As always, the strategy is to find a way of using their strongest representational system whilst involving their other systems to strengthen them. Some children could benefit from creating the table with magnetic numbers on a board, using different colours, perhaps, and arranging the lines in a way which made most sense to them. Some might find it helpful to 'write out' the table in the air in large numbers, pretending they are doing so with sparklers and closing their eyes after each line to 'see' it imprinted on their eyelids while also, perhaps, saying it to themselves. Others might like to write the table out repeating it as they do so. Another approach would be to make the multiplication table out of clay or plasticine, again involving the other systems by training perception or by repetition or listening to a tape.

Of course, *learning* tables is one thing, *understanding* the maths involved and their purpose is quite another. While it is useful to be able to manipulate figures quickly using multiplication tables, if children do not understand the concept of multiplication and why learning tables saves time and tends to increase accuracy, then the benefits gained by learning them are greatly diminished.

Developing creative writing

It can sometimes seem quite a daunting task to help children develop into independent writers who can plan, set out and complete a story or other piece of creative writing. This process can be aided by considering two different aspects of the task:

1. the steps needed to develop creative writing overall;
2. the steps involved in tackling each particular piece of work.

Often children experience undue difficulty because some of these steps have been overlooked and they have been asked to complete a task without sufficient support or experience, or to tackle one which is inappropriate for their developmental stage. Let us look at these points in more detail.

1. Before children can express themselves creatively in written form they must first be able to tap into their imagination, to think, discriminate and organise their thoughts coherently. Without sufficient practice at pretend play, playing with ideas, imagination and words, looking at books and listening to and talking about stories children are unlikely to be able to produce their own creative writing. Although some children will have plenty of experience of this before school some will not. Some juniors will still lack sufficient experience of this kind. Plenty of imaginative play, talking, listening and thinking are thus the essential foundation for independent writing.
2. Each piece of work will also require a number of steps before and after writing. These include:

   - finding a way into the imagination, a way to unlock creativity;
   - time to discuss, play with ideas, brainstorm possibilities;
   - time to think, discriminate, and arrange points in order;
   - writing, a paragraph at a time:
   - reading and checking: read from left to right, top to bottom for meaning; from right to left and from down up, for spellings.

   If insufficient attention is paid to these steps the process and result are usually unsatisfying as in the following example. A reception teacher set the following task which skipped some of the steps needed for a particular piece of work. It may also have been inappropriate for many in regard to point 1 above. She wrote up the model sentences, 'Jack likes jumping', 'Sarah likes skipping'. After asking several children for examples orally, the teacher asked the children to write five sentences using those on the board as an example and to draw a picture for each. Although some children managed, many did not since preparation had been insufficient. As a result, there were a lot of questions to the teacher, some disruptive behaviour from some children who were unable to tackle the task and few sentences written. The demands on the teacher were very great and it was difficult for her both to maintain order and to stay calm.

   If the children had received adequate preparation the task could have been more accessible; the process would have been more enjoyable and satisfying for all concerned and the results superior. One way of doing this follows.

1. The teacher tells the class they are going to make a book about what they like doing to show other classes and parents.
2. Pictures of children performing various actions could be used to introduce the structure, the children guessing what they are doing. As well or instead of this, the teacher could ask the children what they like doing. Another way would be for the children in pairs to ask each other what they like doing and tell the class what their partner likes.
3. The class then plays charades, children miming actions and the others guessing what they like doing. The teacher writes up some of these sentences as a model.
4. In pairs the class builds up sentences using a word pool given to each pair.
5. The children write some sentences, either copying those they have built with the word pool, or making up their own.
6. They illustrate their work.

Some children would probably not be able to tackle stage 5. They would build the sentences and do the illustrations. The work could then be made into a class book which is shown around other classes and then displayed.

Finding a way into the imagination

This may be something concrete, for example, toy figures, a stage set, an idea or situation, a sentence, a piece of writing. It is helpful to present ideas in ways which might engage everyone in the class, in other words, using all three representational systems. For example, if writing a story in a wood, ask the children to think about what it would really be like in a wood. (If not all the children have been in a wood then they could think of a park or garden they knew.) This could be done with the whole class or in small groups or pairs. What could they smell in a wood? What would the scents be if it had just rained or if it was hot and dry? What would the ground feel like under their feet? Might it be soft and springy, covered in leaves, rocky? What might the air feel like? Would there be a breeze or would it be still? Would it be cold or hot? What could they hear: birds, a chain-saw, children playing, an aeroplane, silence, a stream? What might they see around them: trees, undergrowth, little paths leading away, wild flowers, openings in the trees, and so on?

There are many other ways of engaging children's imaginations and of giving them the chance of playing through a story in order to make it real for them. A story board with magnetic or felt figures where children can create scenes, play out stories and talk about what is happening is one of them. Clay or plasticine can also be used as a means for concrete play which inspires the imagination. Or a creature from junk modelling could become the main protagonist in a story. Another idea is to make stage sets as the backdrop against which dramas take place. This can easily be done by cutting cardboard boxes to form a stage and painting them as required, as desert, rain forest, haunted house, etc. If this is not possible then pictures on the wall can be used as a backdrop. The children themselves then use figures to create a story in pairs, or small groups. This would involve talking and playing out the events.

What happens next depends on the child, his or her developmental stage, and teacher or helper time available. Some children might be able to follow a structure similar to the one given below to write fairly independently. Others might build sentences from a word pool first, asking for any specific words needed. Working in a group, children might at times help each other write or have a scribe for the group. This could sometimes be a child from an older class. Groups could also tape their story. Some might tape their story individually or tell it to an adult who writes it down. Taped stories can sometimes be typed up later by a willing parent or helper. Children learning English as an additional language might tape stories in their mother tongue or tell an adult who writes it down. This would contribute to a body of literature in that language for any children who share it.

Sometimes it is necessary to free children from the necessity of telling the truth, encouraging them to draw on the imagination instead. Many older pupils have scored poorly in modern language oral exams for this very reason, remaining silent because they were trying to answer truthfully a question about where they went on holiday or what they did at the weekend. If they understood that the test is to show competence in the language rather than to be truthful, then they could often answer fully.

This point was made very clear once when a colleague and I were working with a group of children learning English as an additional language who were beginners in literacy. On the Monday morning we had started by asking the children what they had done at the weekend. Although many of the children were quite fluent orally there was relative silence, with only the odd answer proffered. Indeed, a truthful answer could be problematic: to those with particular difficulties in their home lives this could seem a very intrusive question; others might simply feel embarrassed if they had done very little. However, when I changed the question to 'What *didn't* you do at the weekend?', with the example, 'I didn't go to the moon' the answers came flowing in. The children spoke more and in a more animated way than they had ever done before in lessons. There was also a lot more humour and enjoyment. Once they were tapping into their imaginations and humour, the children were freed from struggling with the truth about their weekend and gained in confidence. The subsequent written work was the best they had ever done.

A structure which helps many children gain a sense of shape in a story is one developed from the idea of Mary Clay. To do this, fold a piece of paper to make six boxes. Each box is to contain different information in the story:

1. Who the story is about.
2. Where it takes place.
3. What starts off the events.
4. What happens next.
5. The exciting bit.
6. The ending.

This format lends itself to many activities at different levels. A structure of this kind has been found helpful for children with SpLD. Some ideas include:

- Independent writing of stories developed earlier. This might be just one or two words and a picture, a whole sentence, or more extended writing, with the pictures separate and the writing in paragraphs. The structure can, of course, also help children create these stories orally.

- Drawing the pictures and selecting appropriate sentences, or using word building to create a sentence.
- Talking about well known stories and seeing how they fit, or not, into this model. Perhaps writing and illustrating them using this format. For example, Little Red Riding Hood, Sleeping Beauty, Cinderella.
- Sorting out pictures from a story, or pictures and words, or just words into order.
- The class is divided into six groups, each group being responsible for writing one section of the story. This can be done over a week, one group a day continuing the story which is written on large sheets of paper hung in the classroom. This can help children understand how to develop an element of suspense. At the end of the week each group illustrates their own section for a class book.

Another idea to help develop a sense of completing a whole story and build confidence is to take a story book with interesting pictures and stick blank paper over the writing. In a group, or individually, or with the whole class, discuss the pictures and what might be happening in them. Elicit writing for each picture. Tape or write this down, print it out on a computer and stick it into the book so that, from a very early age, children have begun to write real books. This can, of course, also be done with much older children as well.

Working with boys

Recent research into the differences in the structure and functioning of the male and female brain back up what many teachers already know: that boys and girls learn differently. This is not always predictable since there is, of course, considerable individual variation so that some girls will approach learning in ways more common to boys, and vice versa. At present, concerns focus mainly on the underachievement and often growing disaffection of boys. The reasons for this are complex and are in part connected to changes in society and variations in types of work available. This may ultimately require structural changes in the education system as a whole. However, for teachers it may be fruitful to consider in what ways boys tend to learn differently from girls, what their subsequent needs are in the classroom and what the individual teacher can do about this. Failure to acknowledge or understand gender differences can have serious consequences regarding child achievement and also levels of disruptive behaviour in the class. Reported in the *Guardian* (8 January 2000), David Moore, Head of Behaviour Policy at OFSTED, pointed out that boys are currently ten times more likely to be expelled from primary schools than girls. It was noticeable in observing and interviewing teachers for this book that boys accounted for most incidences of disruptive behaviour and loss of motivation. That is not to say that girls do not disrupt the class but, in general, there are fewer of them.

In *The Intelligent School* (1997), MacGilchrist *et al.* pinpoint three differences in the ways girls and boys learn:

- they respond differently to the same stimulus or situation; girls tend to consider the context and think about fundamental details before making a judgement on a moral issue; on the other hand, boys are more likely to make up and stick to rules before deciding;

- girls are generally more 'field dependent', in other words, they are interested in the context and relevance of issues discussed, whereas boys are usually more 'field independent', interested in the concepts for their own sakes;
- girls tend to help and cooperate with one another more, boys are more likely to work side by side without cooperating or to compete.

In their book, *Why Men Don't Iron* (1998), Anne and Bill Moir draw on a wide range of research to illustrate different behaviour resulting from the differing brain structure and functioning of men and women. As they put it, 'Boys and girls have different aptitudes because their brains are specialised for different skills' (p. 126). Some research findings they quote indicating differences in boys' brains and behaviour include the following:

- Boys have ten times more testosterone than girls – they are more aggressive, impatient and competitive than girls.
- Boys aged between 7 and 10 typically spend half as much time on a task as girls do.
- Boys get bored more easily, interrupt each other more often and are far less sociable than girls.
- Boys are less compliant than girls. They do as they are told less readily and less often than girls.
- Boys play in larger groups, their play is rougher and takes up more space.
- In a group, boys interrupt each other, issue commands, make threats and revel in annoying each other. They like jokes and insults and are far quicker than girls to use physical force.
- Boys excel in areas that require three-dimensional thought processing.
- Boys' brains have stonger connections within each half of the brain while girls have stronger connections between the two halves of the brain. This means that girls excel in verbal skills.
- There are 13 mathematically gifted boys to every one girl.
- Tests measuring electrical activity of the brain show that women pay attention much sooner than men. As far as school is concerned, this means that boys will need a greater stimulus than girls in order to pay attention and find something interesting. When boys are unstimulated, the part of the brain which controls behaviour, the cerebral cortex, is not engaged. As a consequence, they are ruled by the limbic system which is emotional and impulsive and can lead to antisocial behaviour.
- Boys are more likely to take physical risks and engage in dangerous activities than girls. Being bored more easily, boys seek ever stronger stimuli in order to feel stimulated. This craving for stimulation can make it difficult to sit quietly and listen or learn to read, etc., rather than moving around and doing.
- Because of their biology and brain complexity, boys are more prone to developmental and learning disorders: four to five times more boys are autistic; three times more suffer from stuttering, four times more are dyslexic, twice as many are mentally retarded and four times as many boys as girls are afflicted with Tourette's Syndrome (TS). Research into the incidence of ADHD is controversial, some researchers claiming nine times more boys are affected, others only four times as many, a few suggesting levels are equal.

Consequences in the classroom

It is helpful if teachers understand that when boys are being noisy, boisterous, competitive and when their attention span is lower than that of girls it is likely to be not because they are being wilfully 'naughty' but because it is the way they are. The behaviour in itself is understandable, the problem emerges because it is often inappropriate in the present-day classroom.

In some ways, schools have perhaps become more suited to the way in which girls tend to learn and behave rather than boys. This is exacerbated in primary schools by the lack of male primary teachers: the environment has become feminised and this may not benefit many boys in schools, particularly as they grow older. It may also be the case that teacher expectations regarding boys can at times exacerbate situations. For instance, a new teacher to a Year 5 class singled out one boy for criticism. He had been seen chatting once, but from then on the teacher made frequent negative comments about his behaviour. The boy was tall, mature, articulate and humourous. To anyone who knew him he was generally law-abiding, sensitive and kind. The new teacher, however, had made an assumption from his appearance that he was a 'troublemaker'.

Rather than berating boys for the way they are, it may be more fruitful to consider how teachers can restructure activities to suit them better. As discussed in greater detail in Chapter 5, behaviour is seldom random. If boys are resorting to disruptive behaviour or failing to flourish it probably indicates that teaching strategies could be better adapted to fit their needs. This again emphasises the need for teachers and teaching to be flexible and eclectic, in other words, drawing on a range of approaches and techniques to engage individual children.

Getting the best out of boys

As one teacher in Year 2 put it, 'If I give the class the task of writing about the experience of looking at, smelling and biting with a crunch into a juicy, red apple, feeling the texture on your tongue, and the juice trickling in your mouth I get very little from most of the boys. With some of them I can see their eyes glaze over. If, however, I tell them to imagine they go to the fridge to get something to eat and when they open the door a hand comes out and grabs them, I get some exciting pieces of writing. The girls can do both.' Martin Spafford, a teacher in a comprehensive school in East London, states, 'Boys need an immediate sense of achievement, and if they don't get it they switch off. Boys need the rewards of a structured framework that measures them and allows them to measure themselves against others, without it they don't care' (*Independent Education Supplement*, 3 April, 1997).

Some approaches which can help get the best out of boys include:

- Structure: many boys seem to benefit from a firm structure. In other words, they like to know where they are going and how to get there. This entails giving clear, often written instructions and including enough steps along the way to give guidance. This does not mean they cannot develop independence and responsibility, but there needs to be enough signposts along the way. They also need clear boundaries, behaviour being reinforced in a firm yet kindly way.

- Attention: they often require frequent attention to keep them on task and a lot of encouragement.
- Frequent changes in the kind of activity in the classroom.
- Interesting work which will give them a sufficiently big stimulus to engage them.
- Boys tend to vie with each other, or against themselves so that they can 'test their strength' in one field or another. In other words, they need successive small targets or projects and an immediate sense of achievement. Children need to achieve frequently. Do this for all and all will benefit, boys and girls.
- Opportunities to let off steam and use up energy: some form of sport, football, running, skipping, games before school, at break and at lunch time, even when it is wet.

2. Encouraging active participation

The two major motivating factors for children in school are, as Marland (1975) notes, achievement and the quality of relationship with the teacher. A third aspect to be considered is that of independence, that is to say, the degree of responsibility children have towards their own learning. A lack of independence can result in children becoming rapidly frustrated and disaffected. At the very best, they fail to develop skills which are crucial for adult life. It is, therefore, helpful if the individual teacher can create opportunities for students to have as much influence as possible over how learning takes place. This is, of course, within the context of clear instructions and adequate structure. It is not a question of leaving children to flounder unaided, rather one of gradually increasing the opportunities for making decisions and taking responsibility.

Many of the strategies in this book deal with ways of training children to study effectively. The aim is for them to become as independent in their learning as possible through mastery of the relevant skills. The teacher remains in charge of the overall process, and within that, the child has the chance to make decisions and take responsibility for his or her own study. Rather than the teacher exhorting children to learn, he or she sets up activities so that children take a very active part and *cannot help but learn since the process is interesting and enjoyable.* Collaborative group work is one technique which can provide variety and can be effective in nurturing motivation, *if it is carried out with sufficient thought and planning and there is sufficient structure, feedback and sense of personal achievement to benefit all.*

One way of helping maintain motivation among children working at a higher ability level is to provide them with the opportunity of working more independently. One idea is to give them a special folder into which they could put any extra piece of work they chose to do in connection with the topic or concerning anything of particular interest to them. This might include stories, poems, factual writing, interviews, illustrations, surveys, measuring, map work, and so on, plus art and craft projects not for the folder. The children could work alone or in pairs and they could show the head teacher their special work each half term.

Creating an atmosphere which supports creativity

Rooms are often far from ideal but, given these limitations, what kind of atmosphere can be created with music, colour, drapes, plants which might support children in their work? How can the children make it their own space so they find it inviting, interesting and yet peaceful enough to help them concentrate? How can the immediate environment of the room become a part of the learning process, relevant to each topic? The children can, for example, be made responsible for the displays in sections of the classroom. This might follow a class discussion about the current topic. The decisions of what to put where, however, would be taken by the children, with help and guidance from the teacher.

The children can also have their own class noticeboard or table where they display items of interest, pictures they have painted at home, information they have discovered and would like to share, and so on. A group could be responsible each week for sorting out and arranging this space.

Working partnerships

The ideas of working partnerships can be developed in several ways. Writing partnerships, for example, have been discussed earlier in this chapter. It can also be useful to create a buddy system in which children who find certain activities in any area of school life relatively easy are paired with those who experience greater difficulty. This does not mean the children have to sit together in class, but they come together at certain times to work on specific projects.

3. Relevant, accessible activities

Giving coherence and a sense of purpose

As the teacher, you have the overview of the term or week's work. You may well have sketched out the plan and can see the relevance of various activites and their importance to the whole scheme of things. You also gain a sense of what ground has been covered and what comes next. You get a picture of how the curriculum builds on what has gone before. The children are usually totally unaware of all this. Consequently, it is often easy for them to think activities are rather arbitrary, that they are doing them simply because the teacher tells them to, that they have no intrinsic value or purpose, that there is no point. Over time, in particular, this can become very demotivating. At worst, especially if there is a disagreement with the teacher, it can easily become a power of wills: 'If the teacher wants me to do it, I'm not going to bother!' At best, this approach denies children the opportunity of having a part in deciding what they learn and a sense of purpose regarding their work. After all, as far as they are concerned, unless they are consulted and have a real say in things, what is it all for? 'Getting a good job' may well have little meaning at 6, or even at 11. So why should children work hard at school? Let us consider some possible reasons:

- to please their parents or carers;
- to please the teacher;
- because they are frightened of consequences from parents and/or the teacher if they do not;

- because learning is a part of life, it is what you do;
- to keep up with or to try to be the same as peers or siblings;
- because they are interested in a particular topic and want to know more;
- because they enjoy the process: for example, exploring ideas, writing stories, working with number, painting, music, dance, being part of the class, working in groups;
- because they enjoy a sense of achievement;
- because they are sure what they want to do in life and know they need certain knowledge and skills for this.

By building good relationships with the children teachers can increase the likelihood of them wishing to please. They can also endeavour to activate their interest, perseverence and enjoyment and help them perceive their progress and appreciate important moments in their process of learning and understanding.

When children repeatedly have to stop one activity they are involved in in order to start something totally unconnected, it tends to demotivate since their choice and independence are undermined. They may well have to rush a piece of work or leave it unfinished because the timetable demands a change of activity. This denies children the satisfaction of a job completed properly and can lead to disaffection. If, however, topics are integrated the sense of having to complete a number of unconnected rather meaningless tasks is diminished. If, for example, the topic is 'Our Environment', what science topic would fit best? If the school has a pond, maybe work on pond life or water. Maths work might include looking at local shops, doing a survey for presenting as a bar chart, looking at prices, and so on. Or it could involve drawing a plan of the room, playground or part of the school.

If children have an understanding of why they are learning something and how it can help them, school work can seem more real and less abstract. Children also like to have an impact in the world, to create and to do things which make a contribution to others: they like to feel successful and powerful. Carefully planned, real activities, therefore, can often be of great benefit. See below for some ideas.

Making the curriculum accessible: engaging the child
One challenge facing teachers using a formalised curriculum is how to engage children in a topic. The need for coherence and a reason for learning has been considered. Another challenge is how to enthuse children in a topic for which they hold no intrinsic interest. Not all children will be excited by the prospect of learning about teeth, the local environment, clothes, the rain forest, Ancient Greece. How, therefore, can the teacher engage and inspire those 30 plus individuals in the class in subjects which may mean nothing to some, bore others and about which others still might already be extremely knowledgeable? Since, as mentioned earlier, delivering a curriculum without taking the children with you is a thankless and pointless exercise, it can be helpful to think in terms of how to engage and inspire. Some suggestions follow.

The process
Most people like to feel powerful. Power is often misunderstood since so very often it is abused and is exerted in a way which crushes others. Here we are referring, however, to a sense of power within oneself rather than power over others. Another way of

expressing this might be to talk of feeling confident doing something and enjoying that process since it adds to your sense of confidence, self-esteem and general well-being. If the process of learning is such that it helps children experience this sense of power within then they are likely to engage enthusiastically in any topic chosen: the process itself will inspire them to greater efforts. If this is the case, then the question remains, what are the essential elements of such a process? Some of these are included below:

- the children have a real part to play;
- the children have the opportunity for being creative;
- the children can experience a sense of satisfaction at completing a task and/or progressing in some way;
- the task is of value;
- the process is valued;
- the product is valued;
- the overall experience is enjoyable.

Starting with the child
Some useful questions to consider with the class when starting a topic might include:

- What do they already know about the topic?
- What do they want to know?
- How does the topic relate to them?
- Why should they find out about it: what can it give them?

Some useful questions to ask oneself might be:

- How can I use all five entry points to engage everyone?
- How can I use language reflecting all three representational systems in order to speak to every child?

Real activities
Book-making is often more engaging than completing worksheets and filing them away. It is generally more real, purposeful, creative and satisfying. It also integrates artwork and sometimes design and technology in making a cover. Books can be made individually, in pairs, in small groups or by the whole class. A class or, indeed, the whole school could have an annual exhibition of books made by the children.

An exhibition of the children's art could be staged at the same or a different time. Children could make a catalogue for the visitors to use giving some information about the pictures and models. This could be linked in to a visit to a local gallery. Gallery staff could be invited to the exhibition.

The children could produce their own magazine. This might be overseen by a parent after school or at a lunch time. Children could contribute articles, pictures, stories, puzzles, etc. they had done at home, or could put forward school work. Children's book reviews could be included.

There are many opportunities for children to design materials for use by each other or other groups of children. For example, older children in the school could make materials or books for the younger ones. Or children could write instructions about how to make something for another class to carry out. Members of that class could then feed back how effective the instructions were so that the children could reflect on the process and refine their work.

Taped resources could also be made. Children learning English as an additional language could make mother tongue tapes welcoming others sharing that language into the school and giving basic information that might help them settle in despite little English. Tapes could also be made in English or a mother tongue about stories, maths or science work. There could also be tapes or a book made by children on how to tackle bullying, giving examples from their own experience. Video presentations could also be made.

There are many ways in which links can be developed with the local community. For example, children could interview local people on a number of topics. In one school some of the children made museum guides of a local museum. Others have provided posters and pictures for dentists, health centres, hospitals and old people's homes in the vicinity.

Links can also be made with classes in other schools in Britain or abroad. This can create a real reason to communicate news, and can help learning to be interesting and purposeful.

Linking abstract concepts to real things which interest children can enhance motivation and understanding in maths. For instance, fractions can seem very abstract concepts difficult for many children to grasp. Concrete examples can help. The act of dividing up bread, fruit, cakes or bars of chocolate usually has real meaning for children. Plastic or playdough food can also be used.

Minus numbers readily lend themselves to work with borrowing sweets, fruit, marbles, etc. A child can be given 'sweets' on the understanding that he or she will pay them back. This child then has minus 'sweets', since the first ones he or she then gets must go to pay back the debt.

Number bonds can be explored by getting children into groups of the target number. How many ways can they divide up into two groups?

If children have used and manipulated mathematical concepts in real situations in small groups where they can explore and take risks without the fear of getting sums 'wrong', they are more likely to gain both confidence and understanding. Harnessing knowledge gained in this way in order to complete written sums usually presents little difficulty: the groundwork has been done, strong foundations of understanding and confidence have been laid.

This chapter has dealt with:

Helping children feel successful as students

- Finding a way in
- Enabling learning
- Specific learning difficulties
- Helping children find the best learning strategy
- Developing story writing
- Working with boys

Encouraging active participation

- Creating an atmosphere which supports creativity
- Working partnerships

Relevant, accessible activites

- Giving coherence and a sense of purpose
- Making the curriculum accessible: engaging the child
- Real activites.

Chapter 3

Working at relationships: making relationships work

A little bit of fear, even if it is caused unconsciously, can go a long way.
(Kathleen D. Ryan and Daniel K. Oestreich,
Driving Fear out of the Workplace, 1998, p. 4)

Humans have already changed the world several times by changing the way they have had conversations . . . Now it's time for the New Conversation.
(Theodore Zeldin, *Conversation*, 1998, p. 7)

'Build a good relationship with the class' you may be told. The question is how. This chapter considers five different aspects of relationships in the classroom:

1. Starting to build relationships and their importance.
2. Fear or trust?
3. The potential power of communication.
4. The nature of the teacher–pupil relationship.
5. Facilitating cooperative relationships in the class.

When making GCSE option choices in Year 9, pupils are often influenced by the quality of relationship they have with their teachers. In other words, if they get on badly with a teacher they are less likely to choose that subject, especially if they are likely to have the same teacher the following year. This is the case even if it is a subject they had previously liked. Relationships count for a lot. This is perhaps even more true in primary schools since most of the week is spent together and the children are younger. The impact you, the teacher, can therefore make on the life of a child in your class is very great. Although relationships may seem just one more thing to think about when there is already so much, they are nevertheless fundamental. They cannot be ignored. At the very least, good enough working relationships with the children in your class will certainly make your working life easier and more rewarding. At the very best, they can help children develop and flourish.

1. Starting to build relationships and their importance

Obviously no two relationships are exactly the same since everyone is an individual. The teacher's task of forming a good relationship with a class is, therefore, a complex one since he or she has to make contact with some 30 individuals at a time. Everyone will have his or her own way of going about this. However, some guidelines which might be helpful when starting to teach follow.

- Learn the names of your class as soon as possible.
- Make eye contact with everyone as soon as possible; until you have spoken to a child by name and made eye contact the personal relationship has not really begun.
- If possible, make the first interaction you have with a child a positive one, perhaps one you initiate, rather than one in which you respond to poor behaviour.
- Notice how pupils sit, stand, move, talk, set about tasks and relate to classmates; what does this tell you about their confidence, level of self-esteem and motivation? What might the world look like to them? How might things sound to them? How might they feel in school? How might you appear to them?
- Notice who is friends with whom.
- When appropriate, show an interest in the children at breaks and after school to get to know them better; chat about their work to find out what interests them and what they like and dislike.
- Try to get a sense of the tone you can adopt with them; what is the most effective way of commenting on behaviour and giving praise and constructive criticism to each child? Although all children need an approach which focuses on praise and encouragement rather than blame and criticism there are, nevertheless, many different ways of addressing the individuals in the class. Some children enjoy humour, others will be confused by it; some respond well to a teacher pointing out quite bluntly that a piece of work is not up to their usual standard, others will take this too seriously and work better with a gentler approach. Remember you probably cannot get the right tone for everyone all the time. Indeed, even *trying too hard* to get it right is unhelpful. All you can do is develop your own confidence, observe keenly, trust your intuition and do what seems reasonable at the time.
- Gradually find a way of making each child feel special, accepted by you and valued, even if you dislike his or her behaviour some or even much of the time.

The fact that it is helpful to trust your intuition and to go by what seems reasonable in dealing with a particular child might mean that, for example, you do not hurry to get eye contact with a certain pupil and wait to build up trust by simply being in the class together for some time before picking him or her out for special attention. Guidelines always need to be flexibly applied when dealing with people.

Cultural differences

It is often helpful to remember that there are many cultural differences regarding attitudes to gender and styles of speaking which can lead to misunderstanding. Even though pupils may be using English words, if their manner and style of speech differ from that of the teacher, good working relationships may be more difficult to develop. Norms of politeness, for example, are culturally based and misuderstandings can easily occur, particularly when people are using the same language but different codes of courtesy. Sometimes children may appear offhand, rude or uncommunicative simply because of cultural differences. The possibility of conflict arising from linguistic mismatches of this nature requires a separate study and is beyond the scope of this book other than to highlight it as an area of potential difficulty.

Emotional intelligence

In her book *Towards Emotional Literacy* (1999), Susie Orbach defines emotional literacy as, 'the attempt to take responsibility for understanding our personal emotions' (p. 2). The concept has been popularised by David Goleman in his book *Emotional Intelligence: Why it can matter more than IQ* (1996) and relates to the inter- and intrapersonal intelligences of Gardner's model of seven intelligences described in Chapter 2. Forerunners of Goleman, Peter Salovey and John Mayer (1990) set out five major domains which make up emotional intelligence:

- knowing one's emotions;
- managing emotions;
- motivating oneself;
- recognising emotions in others;
- handling relationships.

Clearly ability in these domains would greatly support children's academic achievement in school as well as being invaluable for later life. Indeed, Goleman proposes that emotional intelligence is perhaps more important than social class or raw IQ in determining life chances: success at work, quality of relationships and well-being. Many managers today are concerned that young people are unable to collaborate, have trouble receiving criticism and find it hard to interact with colleagues. Some companies are finding the need to train young people in these skills. (Reported in the *Independent on Sunday*, 7 February 1999.)

Any serious attempt to develop an ethos of good citizenship needs, therefore, to be founded in the very basic social skills of working in a team, managing relationships, learning to handle criticism and resolving conflict constructively. These skills, in turn, require an element of understanding one's own emotions and empathy towards others. While schools are not a place for personal therapy, teachers nevertheless have a responsibility to help pupils develop practical skills which are necessary for building and maintaining working relationships in the classroom. At the very least, these skills help children develop confidence as independent learners and contribute greatly to an ordered, smooth-running classroom. At best, they equip children with skills invaluable for their working and private lives. As mentioned in Chapter 1, children cannot flourish academically if they do not experience a good enough degree of emotional well-being within the school.

The pressures of the curriculum are great and, again, it may seem that there is simply insufficient time to think of anything else. There are, however, two points I would like to make.

1. Failing to recognise the central importance of relationships and skills relating to communication and managing emotions is likely seriously to undermine

academic achievement. Ensuring a calm, purposeful environment is also frequently more difficult since unsupportive relationships between pupils often lead to disruptive behaviour. In other words, it is *easier* to teach a class which has developed good, collaborative working relationships and the results are almost certainly superior than if attention and acknowledgement have not been paid to pupils' emotional well-being. Teachers can rest assured that they have not only helped children in the short-term goal of a test result, but have helped equip them with useful lifelong skills. They have also ensured that the experience of being in school will be more pleasant for children and adults alike.

2. The curriculum is the *explicit content* to be 'delivered'. The *process* by which this occurs, however, can be a vehicle for much more. That is to say, much of the development of skills in emotional intelligence can be integrated *implicitly* through the types of activities adopted in the process of helping children learn. Many of the activities suggested throughout the book will encourage the development of collaborative learning through which many aspects of emotional intelligence can be addressed.

This and the subsequent chapter in particular, address these issues.

2. Fear or trust?

An atmosphere of fear

For some time now the business world has been considering ways of improving people's attitudes to work, their commitment, enjoyment and subsequently their performance by considering the emotional atmosphere of the workplace. It has been found that organisations in which people are afraid in some way, afraid to speak out, have new ideas, discuss certain issues, afraid of repercussions, afraid of redundancy, and so on, tend to experience certain problems absent from or less acute in companies which are more open and trusting. These problems include the frequent loss of good staff, lack of innovation and creativity, stagnation. In other words, *people work more efficiently, more creatively and have greater commitment when they feel trusted and valued than when they feel frightened or intimidated: it is counter-productive to use fear as a management technique in order to keep people working hard.* When there is an atmosphere of fear, people tend to feel undervalued since they are not trusted, and frustrated because there is little room for creativity or personal innovation. They lose respect for management and simply do not give their best. As Kathleen D. Ryan and Daniel K. Oestreich, the authors of *Driving Fear out of the Workplace*, succinctly put it, 'Fear makes people smaller – and less capable – than they really are' (p. 46).

It is interesting that these ideas have not always been transferred widely to schools, neither as far as the staff nor the pupils are concerned. Indeed, it seems rather illogical to think that, although adults work better in an atmosphere of trust and openness, children will not. Maybe there is sometimes a confusion here in thinking that trust and openness would necessarily mean an absence of structure, rules and order as far as children were concerned and would erode a teacher's authority. However, there is plenty of evidence to suggest that, even in primary school, authority is ultimately bestowed upon the teacher by the pupils and has to be earned. There is no reason why a teacher cannot be supremely in charge while maintaining firm boundaries in a trusting and open atmosphere.

An atmosphere of fear is one in which pupils are, for example, frightened to make mistakes because of public criticism or a highly competitive ethos, frightened to tell a teacher about a minor difficulty like forgetting a book or kit, frightened of rather high-handed punishments or of not doing well enough in what have been termed 'important' tests, frightened to ask for help. It is true that some pupils will be anxious whatever happens in class because of their life experience outside school. However, if the classroom is an emotionally comfortable place in which trusting relationships are developed then even these pupils have the opportunity to relax a little. Trust is important. Bentley (1998) writes, 'High levels of trust allow us to be risk-takers, to adapt more speedily to changes in our environment, and to experiment with new ways of solving problems' (p. 166).

Failure to create this kind of atmosphere will probably result in most children doing less well than they could. They will not *flourish*: some will withdraw, others will simply coast, keeping out of trouble yet unable to explore ideas or test out creativity, others will resort to disruptive behaviour. Obviously children cannot change schools in the way employees can seek new employment in more convivial organisations. However, they can and often do disengage, turn off, and lose interest as a result of an atmosphere of fear which erodes trust, self-confidence and motivation.

Let us consider, then, just what creating an atmosphere of trust in the classroom might entail.

Creating an atmosphere of trust with boundaries

The essence of this is perhaps the ability to help all the children feel accepted as individuals, even though some of their behaviour might be undesirable. Some strategies which can facilitate such trust include:

- Clear expectations of behaviour using commonly agreed terms so everyone understands what is required and any sanctions which might follow undesirable behaviour. If children are involved in thinking up or selecting a code of behaviour, as described in Chapter 1, then this can help them feel trusted and valued.
- Letting the children know what to expect each day.
- Listening to children's explanations when difficulties arise.
- Allocating time for talking about issues which affect class relationships, for example, in circle time, during sharing, even the odd five minutes here or there.
- Developing mutual respect between teachers and pupils and amongst pupils.
- Stating a common goal: the children's learning and development. The teacher makes it plain that they are all working together. He or she is on the children's side and it is a partnership in which everyone has a particular role. Ways of letting the children know you are really on their side include celebrating their achievements, helping them through difficulties, being kind during sadnesses and enabling their success whenever possible.

- An approach which accepts difference and values diversity.
- Focusing on giving credit for good work and behaviour rather than on blame for poor work and behaviour.
- A model for taking personal responsibility for mistakes or misdemeanours. The teacher is not afraid to admit mistakes and helps pupils to do the same. This is obviously much easier in an atmosphere of acceptance rather than criticism.
- An atmosphere in which everyone supports the success of others.

Unless the children are more or less with the teacher, and unless the teacher perceives the children as active participants in their own learning and accepts them as individuals, even if he or she disagrees with some of their behaviour, then progress will be hindered. In other words, *unless teacher and pupils are on the same side with common aims and a relationship based on mutual trust there will be a constant underlying conflict which drains the teacher and limits the pupils. Without adequate emotional well-being they cannot grow and prosper. Without mutual trust real progress cannot be made.*

The following is an account from a primary teacher who builds very trusting relationships in her class. It gives her views on the importance of relationships and how she goes about building them.

When I think about discipline I realise that it is all down to having a good relationship with each and every child. Once you have a good relationship you can deal with whatever comes up, but you cannot do anything if you do not know the children or if they do not trust you, if there is nothing to go on. I am not saying that I want to be everybody's friend, I just think you need to be on a good footing. You need to know and understand them and they need to think that, out of the whole school, there is someone who knows them. You might start to get this across by having a little chat with them or by saying something like, 'I know your mummy. She's really lovely. I met her yesterday'. The children you have the trouble with, either because you do not get the best out of them workwise or because you find them a bit tricky to deal with, tend to be the ones who are probably hardest to get to know. Most children are more than happy to get to know you and have a relationship with you but some are hard to get to know. Some do not give you anything for all sorts of reasons: they really do not come and meet you halfway.

I think the relationship has a lot to do with trust. I find it similar to being a mother in the sense that, because your children trust you, they can accept that some days you will be in a bad mood for no particular reason and some days you will be in a good mood. On some days something will be acceptable and on others it will not. It is a question of almost getting to that point with the children in your class. It is not making such hard and fast rules. Some days they will come in in a bad mood and I will have to put up with them, and vice versa. That is all part of it, but underneath it all I would like them to feel that what is intact is a trust like that in a family. The bottom line is that I will always care for them while they are in my class. And nothing, but nothing will alter that. As long as that comes through one way or another then we are all going to be okay. It is a totally unconditional acceptance of who they are: as long as they are with me I am going to accept them as a parent would accept them. I think that is not hard to get across. At some emotional level they need to come in on a daily basis knowing that the relationship is going to be all right. For the children who have difficulties at home in particular it is important that they feel very safe with the relationship, that school will not be a repeat of home. I do not think you can have it any other way.

I do not think you can treat every child in your class the same. I think it would be totally unfair, slightly dishonest and very unemotional because if you were treating every single one the same then you would not be responding to them as individual people. It is because you are treating everyone slightly differently and in some cases a lot differently, depending on the seriousness of their needs, that actually puts the human element into it. And when the human element is there then you have the trust because you have the understanding.

The question of being fair can sometimes be a difficult one, especially when still gaining confidence. The same teacher elaborates further on this point.

P was a very intelligent and eager child with supportive parents. In fact, she had so much enthusiasm that you could hardly keep her under control at times, not because she was a discipline problem but simply because of her energy and enthusiasm. She was there with you the whole time, interested in everything and with a great imagination. She responded to everything the minute you started talking, but she never ever put her hand up. She just could not help it. Enthusiasm took over. One thing I used to do was to tease her about not putting her hand up, but a lot of times I just answered her. Since it was my first year of teaching, I suppose I did not know any other way to handle it so it seemed easier to accept what she was saying rather than to keep reminding her to put her hand up. I did start to question whether this was the right thing to do because I did not allow the other children to do this. I knew in my heart of hearts that, for some reason, I was allowing her to do something I was not prepared to accept from the others. I reflected on this and just watched what happened. In fact, the other children did not mind. They never questioned that this was not right for how I was with P. That was me and P. It was clearly not me and that other child or that one. I can only assume that their acceptance of it was because they felt that what they got was fair for them, because they felt okay with their lot. Since their needs were being met they did not need to complain about somebody else's deal. I think I probably carry on doing these same sorts of things in a way. I think it is just summing up a little person's individual requirements and just getting on with it. I really do not believe you can treat every child the same, it comes back to that.

Touch

For some young children in particular, touch will be very reassuring and can help build trust. They may want to hold your hand in the playground, for instance, or if you are sitting and they are standing they may come very close and even lean on you. For X mentioned in Chapter 5, it was very important that he leant against his teacher's legs when the children were on the mat: this helped him feel secure. Some teachers and schools have a 'no touching' policy because of the risk of allegations of child abuse. This seems unfortunate if you are confident using touch, not everyone is. If you do use touch, remember it should always be light, kind, reassuring and never in anger. It is also worth respecting the fact that some children may not want to be touched, or not always. If you sense some children are reluctant to be touched, do not touch them, ask them first if appropriate, or if you have, for example, put your hand on their shoulder and feel them stiffen, take your hand away and apologise.

Assumptions and expectations

How we expect someone to behave often influences how we perceive and interpret his or her behaviour and there is evidence to suggest that a positive attitude towards pupils is associated with fewer difficulties with discipline.

I observed a teacher giving a very unclear explanation and inadequate demonstration of a new swimming stroke. The children struggled across the pool as best they could, clearly not understanding the instructions any better than I had from the side. Yet when they had finished, the teacher told *them* off for not listening properly! It is a common enough assumption in some societies that adults are innately 'right' and children and young people innately 'wrong'. This is very unhelpful thinking for a teacher. When I started running workshops for adults who at the end of each session filled out an evaluation form not only on the aptness of my material and clarity of handouts but also on my 'performance', I suddenly understood to what extent I had held this assumption while teaching in schools. If the children carried out instructions poorly I thought *they* had not listened or had misunderstood, whereas if adults did the same I questioned the clarity of *my* explanation! Children as young as six have told me that they have been reprimanded for not listening properly when they have done so but were still unable to understand the instructions. The teacher assumed that they were at fault rather than that the explanation given was inadequate for some. The implications of such assumptions could be far-reaching, resulting in more disruptive behaviour, demoralisation amongst pupils and conflict with teachers.

If we expect a child to cause us trouble he or she is more likely to do so. If we expect a difficult lesson we are more likely to get one. We will communicate our expectation in many ways, verbally, through body language, and unconsciously. Psychotherapist David Mann (1997) gives an example of how, when he began to think more positively about a client in between sessions, the latter, up till then friendless, immediately managed to form a friendship. We are not obliged to *like* everyone we teach. If we monitor our assumptions and expectations, however, we can perhaps use them to the advantage of ourselves and the children in our class.

I at one time worked with two teachers who shared the teaching of a Year 5 class. One was in her first term of teaching, the other had taught for ten years and was deputy head. Their styles and the assumptions they appeared to hold concerning pupils were very different.

The former commented on what the children were doing well, whether it was behaviour or work. She praised them a lot, both for individual and class efforts, and was helping them feel they were cooperative and successful. They took a pride in their work and helped each other. When children were off task in some way she deftly steered them back on course by focusing on an aspect of the work rather than on the behaviour. In other words, she successfully shifted their attention from the behaviour they should not be doing to the work they should. For example, when a child was speaking during instructions she said, 'M, listen carefully and see if you can tell me in a minute what you will be doing next'. With a pupil who frequently got up and started wandering around the room whenever she lost concentration or came to a difficulty, the teacher said something along the lines of, 'Bring me your work, C, and we'll see how you're getting on', or 'Sit down, C, and do the next question and I'll come and help you in a minute'. This teacher seemed to expect the children to behave well, to do what she said and to be involved in the work. They generally lived up to her expectations.

The more experienced teacher, however, focused immediately on behaviour, often making the opening remark, 'Now I don't want any trouble from you today. Especially from you, C., or you, T . . .'. Although she gave praise, she rarely did so without some criticism. In general, she tended to notice what was wrong before she noticed anything done right. She took a more confrontational approach with the girl who frequently left her seat, focusing on her poor behaviour and warning her she would miss her play, have to go to another class or see the head, depending on the gravity of the situation. Usually one of these sanctions was carried out. This teacher seemed to doubt that the pupils would do what she asked and she seemed to expect them to disrupt the flow of the lesson in some way. They very often did.

The atmosphere in the room, with the same pupils, changed very much depending on who was teaching. With the newly qualified teacher it was generally calm, often with a buzz of activity, though quiet at times. Although there was probably more actual silence during sessions with the experienced teacher this was punctuated by noisy outbursts and conflict. What struck me in particular was that not only did the children seem more interested in the work with the new teacher but there were also *far fewer incidents of disruptive behaviour to deal with*. By focusing on the interest or sense of achievement inherent in completing a piece of work she swept the children's attention along with her away from any possible 'frisson' gained from annoying the teacher in some way. Her expectation of cooperative behaviour added a security which meant the more vulnerable children did not need to misbehave: they felt contained and safe. On the other hand, by focusing on the *possibility* of misbehaving, the experienced teacher seemed to add to the children's insecurity and fear that things might go wrong: she did not contain them. In a sense, she seemed to be offering them a challenge and there were always some children only too ready to take her up on it. Perhaps they sensed an underlying anxiety in her or rose to the occasion of fulfilling her expectations and deep beliefs about them. Or, maybe, at times they just did not like her manner and enjoyed 'winding miss up'.

The basic assumptions we hold about people and the expectations we have about their behaviour shape the way in which we treat them. Consequently, the assumptions you hold about children will significantly influence the way you handle a class. The following assumptions are ones which support the development of an atmosphere of trust with boundaries.

On the whole, most children, most of the time:

- respond well when treated firmly but kindly and with respect;
- want to feel valued and respected;
- want to please;
- respond better to praise than criticism;
- work better when the work is interesting and fun;
- are intrinsically honest and trustworthy when not frightened of the consequences;
- like boundaries which are firmly and kindly maintained.

It is perhaps also worth remembering the power of the pack mentality. In other words, a child alone with a teacher can act very differently from a child among his or her friends or peers. The need to be accepted by the group can outweigh the need to please the teacher. This does not necessarily contradict any of the above assumptions but it can sometimes illuminate behaviour which might otherwise seem out of character in some way.

A cycle of mistrust

By the time some pupils come into your class they may already be demotivated and cynical, expecting very little positive from education in general, the school in particular, and certainly not from teachers. Some may have been labelled early on in their school career as 'problems' and may have come to believe the label themselves. Without redress of any kind, they may have received treatment which seemed to them to be very unjust, and may, indeed, have been so. They may have felt and still feel that no one amongst the teachers is on their side. They may resent all authority figures and expect nothing but the worst from the whole staff.

It is not a question of who is to blame, since this is little more than a red herring when communication has broken down. Both parties may be doing their best to manage in the ways they know and with the skills available to them, but somehow they are not speaking the same language. The result is frequently misunderstanding, conflict and resentment. How can a teacher, as the professional, change this cycle of mistrust and break through a child's resentment and disaffection? What can make a difference?

Obviously it is never possible to change other people, however attractive a prospect that may seem. Nonetheless, it is possible to speak in ways in which it is *more likely* that most children will calm down and *less likely* that they will take offence. How can a teacher remain firm, yet respectful and start to build a trusting relationship? With a large class to contend with, it might seem an unnecessary burden to have to consider the feelings of a child who disrupts, except that, in the long run, it will probably benefit the whole class since disruption will be reduced and it will save the teacher considerable time, effort and trouble. *The aim is to improve the quality of everyone's life.* The following are some suggestions of how to begin building a relationship with a child who has no respect for school, teachers and, probably, him or herself:

- empathise: what does the world look, feel and sound like from his or her position?;
- make opportunities to build the child's self-esteem by ensuring that he or she can achieve tasks, carry out instructions and take responsibility successfully in specific areas;
- take small steps, slowly;
- remain firm, kind and consistent regarding unacceptable behaviour **and** the maintainance of boundaries;
- take nothing personally, neither praise, criticism, nor abuse;
- build a relationship with parents or carers, pointing out the child's successes whenever possible;
- gently contradict the child's unhelpful self-image when appropriate (see Chapter 5 for details).

3. The potential power of communication

With all the pressure of delivering the curriculum it can be easy to overlook the importance of *how* you speak to children. What does your manner convey about how you value and respect them? Certainly, the power of considerate communication and of persistent and consistent kindness, respect, firmness and a steady separation between acceptance of the person and disapproval of unwanted behaviour, should not be underestimated.

Robertson (1981) gives an example of how teachers changing the way they behaved towards a pupil helped him change his behaviour. Robertson also mentions a project by Graubard and Rosenberg (reported by Gray, 1974) in which seven pupils aged from 12 to 15 were taught to treat their teachers differently, responding positively, smiling and so on. After five weeks, the teachers had all started to treat the pupils in a kinder way.

How we say something, our manner, is often more important than what we say. For example, kindly spoken, the words, 'Come here' can be used as an invitation of help or support; shouted in anger, they can be a furious demand. Using words kindly, we can help build the children's self-esteem and optimism and encourage them to flourish; using words harshly, we can undermine and diminish their sense of self. It is a power we have, yet do not always acknowledge.

The last two boys in Year 6 were leaving class at the end of the day. As they left, they knocked over two chairs. The teacher called them back and asked them, politely, to pick up the chairs. They protested that they had not knocked them over on purpose. She said she knew it was an accident, but that she was asking them, politely, to pick up the chairs they had accidentally knocked over. One boy wavered and said to the other that they had better do it. The other, R, refused and started to walk towards the door. The teacher asked him once again, politely, to stay and pick up a chair. As he carried on to the door, she warned him that, if he just walked away now, she would phone his mother, since there had been a history of difficulties and the teacher had agreed to inform her immediately of further problems. R walked out.

Half an hour later the teacher phoned R.'s mother only to find him alone at home. His first enthusiastic response on the phone waned as he realised who it was and why she had rung. The teacher gave him the opportunity to sort the matter out there and then on the phone in which case she would not contact his mother. R agreed and apologised. She praised him for doing so and asked him, in future, to carry out her reasonable requests promptly. He agreed to do so.

What may start out as a small incident may frequently develop into a more serious confrontation since the teacher's power is being tested. If the teacher had ignored the fact that the boys had knocked over the chairs, even though it was an accident, in future they may have felt justified in acting in a similar fashion again. They may well have 'tested' the teacher regarding other boundaries too, and a number of progressively serious contests of will could have ensued until the teacher reinforced a firm boundary.

By picking up on the incident the teacher was reinforcing her expectations of behaviour: mutual politeness and a responsiblility to tidy up after oneself. She did this without jeopardising the relationship since she remained polite and fair, acknowledging that it was an accident and giving R a clear choice with a definite consequence if he refused. Later she gave him another chance, which he wisely took. She was persistent in reinforcing the boundaries she had set and consistent in her expectations of polite, reasonable and fair behaviour. Whenever possible, she offered R a choice, thereby giving him the opportunity to be powerful within the framework she set up, whilst carrying out the consequences she had warned him would follow. When he apologised and agreed to comply in future she praised him.

At the end of the episode R had been given an experience to show the teacher meant what she said and would persist until he complied with the standards of behaviour she set. Since she had remained polite and understanding throughout it was difficult to escape into a 'red herring' of indignation at her manner, and R was left facing the stark consequences of his behaviour. Also, because she had been kind and polite his reaction was one of resignation rather than anger or resentment. He acknowledged that she had 'won'. The teacher had thus reaffirmed her authority without conflict and without damaging, and maybe even improving, the relationship. Future dealings with R would be that much easier.

The teacher's manner throughout made reconciliation more possible. In this she:

- had a positive assumption about the pupil's motives;
- listened to the pupil;
- gave him the opportunity to explain himself;
- gave him the chance to choose a way out and take personal responsibility;
- gave him a second chance;
- adhered to the spirit rather than the letter of the law.

The ability to build helpful relationships with children is not, as we see from an earlier example, always simply a question of length of experience. Indeed, it may well be that those people who are considered 'born teachers' merely have acquired, through life experience, those assumptions about people, expectations of behaviour, focus and communication skills which make for peaceful relationships in the classroom. The fact is, however, that those of us who are not 'born teachers', and I was certainly not among their ranks, need not despair since these techniques can be learnt alongside any other teaching skill. As a rule of thumb, questions to ask oneself might be, How would I feel as a pupil in my class? Would I like to be spoken to in that way? Would it help motivate me or would I feel resentful? How would I feel if I had difficulties with the work? What qualities did I like in my teachers? Obviously, everyone is an individual. However, we might get some very interesting answers to our questions.

It is easy as a teacher to be over-enthusiastic or so intent on delivering the curriculum that we lose sight of the human element, the *people* we are teaching. The pressures can seem very great at times. Indeed, one primary teacher very aware of the need to recognise individuality and build a special relationship with each child observed that she felt under such pressure to get through the curriculum that if a child came and said his mother had just had her head cut off she would have time for nothing other than a brief, 'Oh that's very sad, dear, but now we have to do this . . .'.

Without a good enough relationship, without helping each child feel special, without meeting the pupils and taking them with you, life as a teacher will be much more difficult, less interesting, less rewarding and the education of the children will suffer.

How can we help children feel valued human beings? How can we help each of them feel special? Some of our pupils probably will since they earn our praise easily, they feel valued at home, and can do what is required in the structure of a school. But not all. If you are always younger, told off frequently, never in charge, never 'right', it may be quite easy to feel demoralised from time to time. The years of childhood can seem endless when seen from the child's perspective and for some it may be easy to give up hope. Remembering to make everyone feel special can make a difference. It may be simply a brief word, a warm look, but it can be powerful. It is often paying attention to things which may seem quite trivial to an adult but are very big in the life of a child which help children feel you are on their side, you do notice and do care. One of the most important things of all is to listen.

Listening

A common complaint from children in both primary and secondary who have been excluded from school is that teachers never listen. And it is not just pupils who get into trouble frequently who think that way. A boy in Year 1 who worked well and never gave undue cause for concern regarding behaviour told his mother that there was no point in trying to explain about a misunderstanding 'because teachers don't listen'.

There seems to be a very interesting difference in perception on this point since most teachers would probably claim that if a child comes to them to tell them a concern or to explain about a difficulty they would most certainly listen. Many pupils do not agree, however. Maybe the explanation to this divergence of opinion lies in three differences between busy adults bearing considerable responsibility and children.

1. Children frequently lack a sense of picking the right moment. They may approach a teacher with an important point to discuss just at the moment the latter is about to address the whole class, or is laden with a cumbersome collage, or is sorting out a dispute in the playground, and so on. In other words, children may not choose an appropriate time to speak and assume that it shows a lack of interest rather than a straightforward request to talk about it at a different time when the teacher says something along the lines of, 'I'm busy now, tell me later', or 'Tell me at break'.
2. What may appear of grave seriousness to a child may seem rather trivial to an adult with many other demands.
3. What may seem a very reasonable explanation to a child may appear very different to a busy adult.

Bearing these differences in mind may help erode them. If a teacher explains to the pupils when she or he is likely to listen well, then they may gradually learn the art of appropriateness in this area. Empathising with pupils by trying to see things from their perspective, to feel what it might be like for them and to listen to the words they are using and the way they are expressing them can also be useful, as can sometimes asking pupils to understand an issue from your position or viewpoint, as it sounds to you.

Listening attentively is really a question of keeping an open mind and heart and allowing time for someone to have his or her say.

How you talk matters

In any class, it is likely that children will have strengths in any of the three different representational systems outlined in Chapter 2, visual, auditory or kinaesthetic. Unless deliberately using words from the other two systems, a teacher will probably be operating in only one of those channels, thereby having less contact with a large proportion of pupils. This can lead to a number of difficulties.

For example, children are less likely to understand instructions or explanations given primarily in a system which is not a main one they use. The six-year-old girl mentioned earlier was told off for not listening when she said she had not understood the teacher's explanation about a science experiment. She later reported that she had been listening but simply did not understand. It is easy as a teacher to attribute a pupil's lack of understanding to the fact she or he has failed to listen properly. It may, however, also be because we have not explained in a sufficient variety of ways in order to make sense to all children. In such instances, further explanations using a different approach and including other representation systems may be useful.

Other difficulties may include less rapport, poorer relationships and an increase in conflict. Bandler and Grinder (1979) report how they noticed that when therapists used a different representational system from their clients the latter tended to feel less well understood and the relationship suffered. They write:

If you want to get good rapport, you can speak using the same kind of predicates that the other person is using. If you want to alienate the other person, you can deliberately mismatch predicates (p. 15).

Speaking in a range of representational systems, on the other hand, can help children listen, understand and feel understood since you are using their own 'sub-language'. Thus it can have a positive influence on motivation. It can help in the establishment of rapport with a class as a whole and with individuals. At times of potential confrontation it might add an extra sense of understanding which could avert greater conflict. Misunderstanding and, therefore, conflict is easier when two or more people are speaking different 'sub-languages' since each feels less well listened to and less understood, whilst finding it harder to understand the other. By encouaging children to describe incidents from their point of view and from their position, and to listen to the words they choose and how they express themselves, teachers can help open up a dialogue. By using a range of representational systems relationships with colleagues and parents can also be improved.

Why frequent shouting can be unhelpful

It is probably true to say that no one enjoys being shouted at and if a teacher relies on shouting as a basic technique for classroom management then this may hamper attempts to build an atmosphere of trust. Like anything else, shouting can become a habit and may not be one which serves you best as a teacher. Relationships with some children may be damaged and their creativity, learning, confidence and motivation may well be undermined. Very frequent shouting also tends to indicate a lack of confidence in the teacher. As Robertson (1981) writes, 'The experienced teacher will avoid bullying, shouting, sarcasm and other such methods, as these really only reveal one's own insecurity' (p. 34).

Nevertheless, most people shout at some time when dealing with a class of children and, at times, it can be effective, especially when reserved for making a big impression, to prevent or stop something dangerous, for example, or to underline the seriousness of an incident. To call for order if a class is noisy some teachers clap their hands, use a small handbell or shake a tambourine to avoid shouting in order to save their own voice and create a different atmosphere.

When starting teaching I was very unhappy about my level of shouting and was painfully aware that I lacked the communication skills, confidence and fluency of classroom management techniques that some people seemed to employ 'naturally'. Fortunately, this can all be learnt.

Unless used rarely for moments of some gravity, shouting is often inefficient. If a teacher shouts frequently some pupils may be unable to hear the instruction or message he or she is trying to get across for two main reasons:

1. the manner of delivery overshadows the message;
2. the children's emotional response to being shouted at prevents them from listening or working well.

Let us consider these in more detail.

1. When a teacher shouts pupils tend to become diverted by the manner of delivery rather than the meaning of the words. In any spoken communication there are always two aspects, the apparent message or content, the actual words, *the explicit message*, and the manner in which they are delivered, the tone of voice, volume, body language, facial expression, in other words, *the implicit message*. Clearly there can sometimes be an incongruence between these two messages as in the case when someone says, 'I'm not angry!' through clenched teeth and with a general body posture and facial expression which suggest the opposite to the words. As human beings we usually respond to the manner of delivery, the emotional charge, *the implicit message* rather than the actual words, the intellectual content, *the explicit message*. When a teacher shouts frequently the children are likely to note little other than the implicit message, something along the lines of, 'Miss/Sir is cross with me' or 'I've done it wrong'. Thus the explicit message, the instruction or comment is, in many cases, probably lost.

2. The class will respond to being shouted at, the implicit message, in various ways depending on their past experiences, personal resources and learnt patterns of behaviour. For some, shouting will be the norm at home and they will, therefore, scarcely notice it unless it is exceptionally loud. As a means of gaining their attention or of impressing them with a particular message it will largely fail on this count too. For others, a shout will often be accompanied by a blow. The feelings of fear, anger or dread these pupils are likely to experience will ensure that they are too involved in their own emotions to pay much attention to the teacher, his or her message, or their work. For other children, shouting will be a rare occurence marking a very serious or dangerous incident. These pupils, too, are likely to be so caught up by their emotional response that they will be diverted from the explicit message and the work in hand.

   If we are shouted at by an authority figure even as adults we tend to revert to patterns of defence learnt when very young, freezing and withdrawing, engaging in rather frantic activity as a panic reaction, or responding aggressively in order to hide our fear. If a teacher shouts angrily at even insignificant incidents some children will also increase their level of disruptive behaviour so as to do something worthy of a shout, thereby making sense of the teacher's response. None of these reactions encourages learning, thinking, understanding or creativity.

If shouting is the norm, after a time, individuals, the class as a whole and other teachers and pupils will begin to think of them as 'naughty', in other words, that they deserve such treatment. As one girl in Year 6 noted, 'They must be a naughty class because miss shouted at them so much'.

Realistically, however, many of us are apt to shout at some time, and sometimes more than we would wish. When feeling overstretched some teachers warn their class that they are likely to shout more or seem cross more easily than usual that day. This enables children to understand that teachers' responses may sometimes be harsher than usual because they are affected by their own feelings rather than because the children have done anything particularly serious. Without such a warning some pupils may become confused at the unpredictable level of a teacher's response. Some may resort to more extreme forms of often disruptive behaviour as a result, others will simply 'turn off' in anger, fear or resentment, or withdraw. It also warns children of the consequences of any misbehaviour so that they have a choice: to go ahead, misbehave and reap the consequences, or to toe the line.

If you have had a bad day without recognising it in advance and without giving a warning and you have at times shouted in ways you later regret, then all is not lost. One primary teacher refers to such episodes as her 'being a gorilla' for a while. In this way she takes responsibility for her own behaviour while helping the children to understand and feel comfortable with it. At a similar time in future they can recognise the 'gorilla mode' and realise that 'Miss is in a bad mood' and that they had better watch out. Warning children before or commenting after and apologising if appropriate also gives a model for talking about and taking responsibility for feelings and behaviour which can be of great value to pupils in school and in later life.

Questions to ask if concerned about the frequency of your shouting
- In what ways can you try to build positive relationships with the pupils?
- How can you show you are committed to helping them and are fundamentally on their side?
- How can you build their confidence and self-esteem?
- What can you do to help each child feel special?
- What limits can you set that would help you feel more comfortable in the classroom? In other words, how can you feel less pressured by the children, so that there are fewer times when you feel like shouting?
- What classroom management techniques could you employ to reinforce these limits? Strategies for entering and leaving the class, perhaps, taking turns, staying seated, and so on.
- How can you think about the class that would help you develop cooperative ways of working together? How can you change your expectations and assumptions?
- What support can you get for yourself? Who could help?
- What alternative classroom management and communication skills could you learn and employ? In other words, what could you do instead of shouting?
- How differently would you stand, sit, walk and talk when using these skills?
- What could you do in order to create a gap between an incident to which you would usually respond by shouting and beginning to shout? This gap provides the time in which you can choose new behaviour.
- When, on occasion, you still shout more than you would like, how can you talk to the children to reassure them about this? How can you reassure yourself?

4. The nature of the relationship

Friendship is a relationship between equals: therefore, teachers and pupils can never be friends as such, since the former holds the power and responsibility and can make judgements which affect the latter. The teacher may be kind, caring, considerate, very warm and friendly while continuing to maintain a sense of being in charge. Keeping this balance can at times be difficult and it can be easy to try to be liked, to care too much or to be too dependent on a pupil's success, ability to change, etc. Remaining aware of your role as the responsible adult is important since children can feel betrayed if a teacher appears as a friend one minute, telling them off or referring them to a higher authority the next.

In loco parentis

The teacher–pupil relationship in primary schools can be a very intense one and this is not surprising when it is considered that the teacher is *in loco parentis*. The role of standing in for a parent can result in children sometimes transferring their feelings and ways of behaving towards one or both parents onto the teacher. It is common, for example, for pupils to call their mothers 'miss', their dads 'sir', and vice versa. The transference of feelings, which are often very powerful ones, can evoke a strong response from the teacher. In other words, the teacher may be invited to respond to the children's feelings of love, hate, irritation, embarrassment, anxiety, etc., expressed through behaviour directed at him or her *but meant for the parent*. Since children are growing up and learning to become independent this process can involve rebellion and anger directed at the teacher: sometimes it is necessary to reject a parent and the old ways of relating in order to become independent. This is aptly expressed in the joke about adolescents:

Question: Why did the teenager cross the road?
Answer: Because his parents told him not to.

Although children of primary age have not yet reached adolescence they are nevertheless involved in a similar process, albeit at a milder level. They are constantly coping with changes in their bodies and in their thinking and are trying out new behaviour, exploring who they are.

It can be helpful as a teacher not to take things personally and to remember that a child may well be responding to your role rather than to you. This can be a rather humbling thought when pupils seem to like you. On the other hand, a period of turbulence can sometimes indicate that a pupil feels safe enough with you to try out new behaviour and develop. This can be rather an unwelcome compliment since the behaviour might be troublesome in some way and it is at times difficult to remember that it is possible only because of the strength of the relationship you have developed.

The example of a well-behaved, mature and able boy, A, in Year 3 illustrates this point. The teacher had stayed with the children in the transition from infants and had worked hard at building strong relationships with individuals while helping them to work together cooperatively as a class. By the spring term of Year 3, she knew the children well and was very popular. It was noticeable at parents' evening during this term that A's work had deteriorated markedly since returning from the Christmas break. The teacher discussed this with his parents and suggested a meeting for the following week at which A was to be present, when they would have more time to talk about what was going on.

Thinking about the whole of A's behaviour and body language before the second meeting the teacher realised that, in fact, he seemed to be experimenting with the image of being 'cool' in class. He had been interested in girls the previous term, was very concerned with presenting a 'cool' image and seemed almost obsessively interested in his gelled hairstyle. The week before he had been leaning back so far on his chair in his desire to appear laid-back and cool that he had actually fallen off! This appeared to be connected to a general insecurity about himself, who he was and his ability to form relationships. He had appeared to feel very rejected when the girl he had a crush on had not reciprocated the term before. His friendships had been stable since reception but now he started rejecting his hitherto closest friend, choosing another boy, N, as his 'best' friend. The latter had taken up the role of class chatterbox and generally produced less work than A.

At the second meeting, the teacher spoke skilfully to A and elicited that he did not want to 'shine' in class, did not wish to be singled out as having done good work and wanted to be just one of the crowd. In fact, he wanted to be N. Alone with the parents, the teacher wisely suggested that this was probably just a phase and that the best course of action would be to observe for a time, letting A experiment for a while before finding a new balance for himself. Knowing him, she thought he would soon become bored with his chosen image. A meeting was planned for after Easter. She was indeed correct, and by the summer term A was working as usual.

This was an interesting episode for several reasons. It illustrates that children are not just learning the curriculum in school but are experimenting with and developing their character, behaviour and habits. It is quite likely that, if A had not felt secure enough with his teacher, he would not have experimented in this way. Yet the gains were very great. Although, from a strictly academic point of view his performance might have dropped for a term, his overall development, his education in a wider sense had progressed greatly and he appeared more confident, happier and assured in the summer than before. The teacher had handled this period sensitively and wisely, trusting in A's own process, communicating with parents and monitoring the situation.

Letting go and taking over

At the beginning of a new year it is often difficult for the children to accept a new teacher simply because the relationship is an intense one. Likewise, it is common for teachers to miss a class that has moved on. It always feels strange at the beginning of a year since new relationships are being formed and, at this stage, may well feel less comfortable and perhaps less rewarding than those formed with the previous class at the end of a year spent together.

A teacher reported how she had been feeling like this when two of her former pupils came to her saying how much they were missing her and could she promise to be their teacher the following year. She was non-committal, saying it was unlikely. She also said that she missed them too, had really enjoyed teaching them and would always remember them, but that things had to move on. She then turned the conversation onto how their new teacher had lots to offer them because he was different and how they would soon enjoy him once they had got used to him. She saw them later that week talking and joking with the new teacher and realised this had already happened. Children are often very loyal. Maybe, it was only once they had paid their dues to their past teacher by saying they were missing her and would like her as their teacher again that they were then able to accept the new one.

Sometimes it can be difficult to see a class with whom you had a really good relationship getting on as well or, it may seem, even better with the teacher who takes over from you. Rather than letting this erode your confidence it may be worth considering two points:

- it may be partly due to the relationships you built up and the way in which you helped the class support each other that the children are able to go on and develop good working relationships with a new teacher quickly;
- whatever anyone offers a class is unique and subsequent good experiences never undermine the connections you developed and the contribution you made to those particular children's lives.

Another aspect of transition is being in the position of the new teacher above, in other words, having to take over a class who have had a close relationship with a very popular teacher. This can be a daunting prospect, especially if you are relatively new to teaching and your personal style is very different from that of your predecessor. It is a time when it can be very helpful to use your support systems well and focus on your strengths as outlined in Chapter 6. It may also be useful to follow the guidelines for making contact with a new class described earlier. It may well be of use to talk about what is going on with the class, that is to say, to acknowledge that it may be a little strange at first because you are different, but that this can offer them something as well.

Managing transition

A very effective teacher was puzzled towards the end of Year 2 when her class became uncooperative. They had been working together well and had seemed, on the whole, helpful, willing and pleasant to her. Suddenly, they were uncooperative, difficult to manage and had lots of conflicts arising amongst themselves. I suggested this change might be connected to the oncoming transition to juniors; in other words, the children might be anxious about moving on to the juniors, perhaps also about leaving their position as the oldest, the top of the school and starting again as the youngest group with least status. They might well be feeling sad at leaving the infants and sad at leaving her. At times of imminent transition such feelings are usually present among large sections and possibly all of the class. Unless they can be addressed consciously, that is to say, talked about, it is likely pupils will act them out in some way, frequently through uncooperative and disruptive behaviour. Since it is often easier to experience feelings of anger rather than sadness or fear, the incidence of conflict might also increase. Pupils who tend to bully others might do so more frequently at such times, endeavouring to force others to express the fear they are suppressing. To a certain extent, such feelings are likely towards the end of any school year when the children are moving on to a new teacher, expecially if the teacher is unknown or is known to be very 'strict' or frightening. Moving from the infants to the juniors and from primary to secondary are, of course, likely to provoke the biggest reactions of this kind.

Once alerted, the teacher started to address the issue in circle time, getting the children to talk about:

- what they were anxious about in going to the juniors;
- what they were looking forward to;
- what they were sad about in leaving the infants;
- what they were glad to leave;
- and what they would like to take with them.

The teacher also shared her feelings that she would miss them all. It was really an exercise in helping the children understand that it is natural to feel sad, angry and anxious at a time of change and that, although they would be leaving behind some things they liked, they would be gaining others in their place. Once they got used to it they might even prefer some aspects of the juniors. Since they were familiar with what they were leaving and the new was more unknown it was not surprising it all felt a little frightening. A number of the fears expressed focused on anxieties about finding their way around the junior school.

The overall strategy of talking about the significance of the change to the juniors seemed to help: since the children could voice their feelings the need to act them out diminished and the awkward behaviour decreased. On the practical side, a visit to the junior part of the school as a whole class had been planned while the juniors were away. After this, additional visits were arranged in pairs at a time, two children from Year 2 being shown round by two members of Year 3.

Another technique for easing the transition is for the class to take something with them that could represent their being together during the stage they are leaving. The class mentioned above had already made a large bowl which served this purpose well. Inside it had a few words and a picture from each child describing something he or she liked to do. The article taken from year to year could be anything suitable, a class book, picture, object, as long as every child contributes in some way.

For those leaving for secondary school it can be particularly helpful if everyone can take home a momento of the class working together. A class book, newsheet or newspaper could be signed by everyone and photocopied. The subject matter could be things they are sad and glad to leave behind, what they would like to take with them and hopes and fears for secondary school. If the content deals with such concerns then the process of creating the momento can act as a medium for discussing issues about the imminent transition. Most schools have some kind of public ceremony for Year 6 leaving; the making and distribution of the class momento could act as a more private, class ritual to mark the ending of a chapter in the children's lives.

Another idea would be to make a class video, each child saying something about his or her time in the infants or in the school. If funding permitted this could also be copied for all class members.

One issue which is commonly present when leaving for secondary education is loss, the loss of friends, teachers, the relative intimacy and cosiness of a primary school in which you are well known, contact with the innocence and relatively carefree existence of early childhood, and so on. One way of managing this material is to consider what the children have gained, in other words, the qualities and skills they have developed which they will be taking with them. Of course, there are the obvious gains in most cases of learning to read, write and develop some mathematical understanding as well as acquiring knowledge and understanding in other fields such as history, geography, art, music, PE, science. Other skills may be less tangible. To varying degrees, the children will have learnt to sit and listen, speak to a large group, cooperate with classmates, perform in front of others, make friends, etc. Although they may not be moving on with all or any of their friends it can be helpful to consider the qualities of those friends and teachers they will miss. In a sense, as in the old adage 'beauty is in the eye of the beholder', the very ability to perceive qualities in another suggests the 'beholder' possesses them too, though maybe in an unacknowledged form. Being aware of this, children can understand that, although they may not be with their friends in the future, they have not lost them entirely, they are different because of having known them and take something of them along with them as they move on to the next stage in their lives.

Relationships with parents and carers

As the teachers quoted earlier this chapter and in Chapter 5 emphasise, getting to know parents and carers can play a crucial part in helping children succeed. For parents, it can often be quite intimidating to have to go into a school and talk to a teacher. I was shocked when my first son started school just how nervous and awkward I felt talking to his teacher even though I had taught in schools for years and was used to working with heads, senior management and classroom teachers! Also I had had, overall, quite positive experiences in school as a child. Imagine how difficult it must be if you have no experience of talking to teachers as an adult and have had a very unhappy time in school yourself. It is up to the teacher, as the professional, to ease the way for all concerned. It can, therefore, be useful to put some effort into developing a relationship with parents and carers as a matter of course before a particular need arises to talk to them. This can be very low key, maybe a smile and a brief comment, not necessarily about their child but if so a complimentary one, before or after school. If parents have a concern they will then find it easier to approach you; and if you have one you have already established some kind of relationship. Misunderstandings are more likely to arise when there is little or no communication between school and home.

Although parents and teachers may sometimes think differently about education they generally have the child's best interests at heart even if they have different ways of working towards achieving this. They are, therefore, on the same side.

In dealing with parents it can often be fruitful to consider how things must seem from their point of view. It is devastating to hear a stream of complaints and criticisms about your child and hard to know what you are supposed to do with this information. Consequently, it is usually helpful to alert parents and carers early on if you are concerned about a child's work or behaviour rather than allowing things to progress too far. Parents are, quite justifiably, often angry if this is not the case. It is usually helpful, too, to praise their child and point out what he or she can do well. It is frequently the case that a child's progress is directly linked to the parents feeling happier about him or her in school. In other words, once the parents relax a little and feel relieved that their child can do something praiseworthy, once there is some hope, real improvements are often made.

Up to the time your own children first come to school, even when they are in nursery or playgroup, you can often still have considerable input into their daily lives. Suddenly they start school and someone else, the teacher, has a very central role in their life and is in charge of what happens to them for much of the week. This can sometimes be a difficult transition for all involved. Parents will have their own expectations of teachers and school depending on their own experience and views. Most will probably want their child to 'be happy' and 'learn', even though there are many interpretations of these terms. As one parent, Debbie Swyer, writes:

> Before my son started school I used to tell him how much I had loved it. Every day something new and unexpected seemed to happen – it was all very exciting and the teachers seemed to share our excitement. I wasn't nervous when he went because I felt very positive about it all.
>
> I think my ideal reception teacher would be someone who could offer lots of learning experiences; someone who'd ask the children lots of questions even if they didn't always know the answers themselves and be as delighted as they could be in what they discovered. I remembered school was exciting and I wanted it to be like that for him too. It may sound rather pompous but I thought an approach like that could give the children the possibility of believing they could fulfill their potential.
>
> My son's first school was a small one. I remember he always wanted to show me things they had been doing in the class and the teacher encouraged us parents to come in and look and admire. Really I can't say I had anything in common with her as an individual, but she was always very professional and all the children seemed very fond indeed of her and each other. She was always very positive and fair to them which I much admired. I guess she was pretty ideal!
>
> When I asked my husband how he had felt about our son going to school for the first time he said that he had wanted a place and a person who could provide a secure environment. He hoped there would be a structure for learning rather than an emphasis on particular achievements alone. He didn't want him to be at a school where only the loudest made themselves heard but somewhere he could be listened to and learn to express himself. Because of his job my husband rarely collected our son from school, so he didn't have the opportunity I had to 'see him in action' but he said that he had always felt good about the school and the teacher because our son spoke so positively about his class and classmates.
>
> Whether the teacher did or did not live up to our expectations – she certainly lived up to our son's.
>
> My son is now a junior at another, bigger school; but our hopes for his schooling have really remained the same. Of course, we want him to be able to read and keep up at maths but the fact that he is still so enthusiastic about his school and his teacher and his classmates; that he wants us to come and see what he has been doing and that his voice is heard, remain the most important things.

5. Facilitating cooperative relationships among pupils

There are many advantages to promoting cooperative relationships. For example:

- The greater the cooperation between children, the less conflict is likely between them.
- If children are angry with each other they may well become angry with the teacher.
- Pupils can help and, therefore, could also hinder each other learn. If the former, more children can succeed and will have a greater investment in making school work for them. Behaviour will improve.
- If children feel comfortable in the class and happy with their peers they are more likely to flourish.

Working with a newly-formed class

A little time spent working directly on relationships may save time in the long run since it can help peers support one another. The suggestions below can be adapted in many ways as appropriate for different ages. There are many games which can be used and some can be found in the Appendices (E).

Another way in which a class can build fruitful relationships is to work on a joint project. There are many possibilities. These include working together on a class assembly, organising a cake sale, running a stall at a school event, making books for another class, or for Year 6 as a goodbye gift, drawing pictures to decorate a local Health Centre or dentist's surgery, writing poems and making a class book to present to an old people's home. Any project in which the children work together, share an experience and create or contribute something and/or can have fun usually helps raise morale and encourages the development of a class identity, a sense of pride at belonging to the class and more harmonious relationships within it.

The teacher quoted earlier in this chapter gives her view on helping a class to bond.

I think it is very important that your class does 'gel'. This process starts to evolve by itself once you begin to get your relationships sorted out. As long as each and every child feels his or her lot is fair, that starts to make it 'gel'. Things are not working if one child thinks that somebody else is getting a better deal. So as long as you have taken care of that with your relationships you have made your first move towards everybody getting on together, because you have taken away that aspect of potential jealousy or antagonism.

For me, the easy thing to help a class get on well together has always been doing circle time. I think this can only start to work once people begin to feel confident, and I think that comes back to feeling okay in the classroom and feeling secure that your deal is a fair one. Then, I think, you can move on from there, though you have to take it quite slowly, especially if it is a class that has not done circle time before. You cannot expect people to start opening up right away about their feelings and their relationships in such a highly public place. The aim of my early circle times has really been just to have some fun and games. You have to accept that it can get noisy and a little bit out of hand. You also need a quiet place to do it in. Once the children get into circle time as fun time and have a sense of being together, you can build up from that.

You need to define what your rules are at the beginning of circle time and this sets your boundaries. One of my first rules is that anything discussed does not go any further than our classroom. I think it is quite a big step for a lot of children to feel that they can say things that are not going to go anywhere else: the circle is a sanctuary and anything they say is not going to be talked about elsewhere. I am quite ruthless about this fundamental rule because it makes it safe. I think the other thing that surprises the children is that we, as a class, can have secrets from other people in the school. This helps the children feel a real class identity.

Once you have established this I think it is quite nice, rather than trying to get the children to expose themselves, to start on something simple, maybe on building someone in the class's self-esteem, so that everyone can start thinking about considering other people's feelings. The children become aware that not everyone is happy or confident in a big group. They realise that they can do something to help someone feel better. All these sorts of things start to build up the trusting part of circle time. Then I think you can begin to work on bigger issues, getting them to talk a little about their own personal feelings. They begin to identify their emotions, distinguishing between anger and sadness, for example. They get to talk about particular emotions and to understand that there are reasons why they are feeling particular moods.

It is also nice in circle time to get children who do not normally talk to each other to try to find things out about each other. I think it is important that the children do get to know everyone in the class, particulary if it is a class that is not bonding terribly well. If this is the case, you tend to find that there are pockets of friends and that is why the class is not bonding as a whole. There will be a number of little groups which are probably all functioning wonderfully as groups, but are not functioning so well as one big unit.

Helping children accept difference and value diversity

The ability to accept difference lies at the heart of cooperative relationships since difference and the fear of it often contribute to conflict. Usually we experience animosity towards two different kinds of people: those who possess qualities similar to our own but which we do not acknowledge or accept in ourselves and those who are very different, their difference challenging our equilibrium since if they are different maybe they are 'better'. In relation to the latter we may experience feelings of jealousy or envy which may or may not be acknowledged. It is generally the case that the less confident a child is and the poorer his or her self-esteem the less tolerant he or she is of difference. Consequently, strategies which help build pupils' confidence and self-esteem will inevitably help them to accept difference and value diversity. Talking about difference whenever relevant and helping the children to think for themselves and make connections concerning the issue can also be of value as the following example shows.

Although classes vary, a sharpened awareness of a range of differences frequently occurs at seven, eight or nine. This was very clear in a Year 3 class when two trends became apparent.

- For a time, the issue of girl and boyfriends suddenly became more important, a boy having a crush on one of the girls. Up till then girls and boys had played together without particular comment about gender. For a while it was impossible for girls and boys to play together without being teased for being girl or boyfriends.
- Another common theme at playtimes during this period was the threat along the lines of, 'If you don't play ——— with me I'm not your friend any more'. Underlying this seemed to be the fear of any difference, that even if someone likes different things they cannot remain a friend.

The upsets in friendships at this time began to interfere with some of the children's learning and the teacher decided to address the issue in circle time, spending half a term on the topic of difference. This included talking about likes and dislikes and simply acknowledging that people are different and friends do not need to be the same in order to remain on good terms. The children could see in relation to others that sometimes quite unlikely people were friends partly because they were so different and that it was often this very difference which made relationships interesting. The discussion was also put in terms of preferences merely being different rather than some things being 'good' or 'bad'. This strategy seemed to help the class work through these issues more quickly than they might otherwise have done and more supportive working relationships developed.

The following exercises can be done with a range of year groups, adopting an approach relevant to the age of the pupils. It is only one way into the topic and is just a beginning. Yet it can provide a reference point at a later date if it becomes appropriate or necessary to touch on the issue again.

Exploring differences and similarities

This work can be integrated into several topic areas, for example, 'Myself' or 'My School'. The children can make a class book or poster about their differences. To start, the class as a whole think of all the differences present between them and the teacher writes them on the board. These differences may include age, colour, race, gender, interests, size, abilities in different areas, experience. The idea is to note differences, many of which will be obvious anyway, in a spirit of acceptance. That is to say, before starting the process the teacher and class will discuss the concept of differences and that they signify merely a difference rather than something which is 'better' or 'worse'. All contributions are to be general and not personal. Class likes and dislikes could be included in this exploration or could be discussed separately.

Children can use this information to write poems or prose or draw pictures illustrating the diversity in the class. One way of setting this in a context would be for them to describe the differences within the class to visiting aliens. They could also explore what it might be like if people were all the same, plants and animals were all the same, and so on. Who or what might they be like?

It can also be pointed out that, despite differences, the pupils share many similarities. These, too, can be considered. For example, pupils share a similar age, they are in the same class, they are all in school with the same number of years to go.

How pupils can support each other

Obviously class members can help or severely hinder their peers' progress in class. The aim of this exercise is to get children to be aware of how they can help each other work more effectively. If it is agreed early on that most children are in favour of supportive, helpful relationships in the class, more pupils will feel supported in discouraging bullying or disruptive behaviour in future from some class members.

Children brainstorm in small groups all the ways in which they can help each other and then ideas are shared, the teacher acting as scribe on the board. Later the ideas can be displayed in the classroom, referred to as necessary, and updated when appropriate.

This approach can be used with group work in mind so that the children develop guidelines which will support them working collaboratively. These guidelines might include:

- Everyone can speak in the group.
- Everyone respects what others say and do.
- Only one speaks at a time while the others listen.
- Everyone works hard.

After group work it can be useful to review how they worked together to see if it was easy to keep to the guidelines, if they should be changed or new ones are needed.

It is easy to underestimate the power of relationships in teaching. It can often seem that personality is set. Our manner in talking to people however, how we treat them and how we communicate are largely behaviours we have learnt. Once learnt, they can be relearnt and altered, new communication skills can be acquired. The way we treat children matters: a relatively small change in approach can result in a considerable difference in the relationship. Directing effort into creating good enough working relationships with each child will make teaching easier and more rewarding and will help the children develop their potential.

This chapter has dealt with:

Starting to build relationships and their importance

- Cultural differences
- Emotional intelligence

Fear or trust

- An atmosphere of fear
- Creating an atmosphere of trust with boundaries
- Touch

- Assumptions and expectations
- A cycle of mistrust

The potential power of communication

- Listening
- How you talk matters
- Why frequent shouting can be unhelpful

The nature of the relationship

- In loco parentis
- Letting go and taking over
- Managing transitions
- Relationsips with parents and carers

Facilitating cooperative relationships among pupils

- Working with a newly-formed class
- Helping children accept difference
  and value diversity
- Exploring differences and similarities
- How pupils can support each other.

Chapter 4

Managing and resolving conflict and anger

Some frustration is inherent in learning and hence some measure of anger is likely to be part and parcel of the situation . . . If there is no one who will tolerate such feelings [anger and envy], it strengthens the student's fear that all aggression is destructive and so powerful that it cannot be dealt with by anyone. He may be driven to inhibit it to a degree where it interferes with outgoingness and achievement. On the other hand, a student less able to control his anger may become increasingly violent in the hope that someone will take him seriously and help him to deal with his aggression by setting limits.

(Isca Salzberger-Wittenberg, Gianna Henry and Elsie Osborne, *The Emotional Experience of Learning and Teaching,* 1983, p. 47)

Conflict and anger in primary schools can manifest in different ways. An argument at lunch time can sometimes continue in the classroom with jibes, notes and even blows being exchanged. Jostling on the stairs or in the cloakroom in the morning may lead to kicking and threats of more at playtime. A dispute about whose turn it is may result in angry words and refusal to speak to each other again. There are many potential incidents. Clearly the time taken up in dealing with such issues, the disruption to classes and the emotional upset usually involved can detract considerably from a calm purposeful atmosphere and can impede progress. Time spent helping children understand and manage their own anger and resolve conflict constructively can contribute significantly to the children's overall emotional well-being and, therefore, their achievement. It can also result in life being much calmer and pleasanter for all concerned. The more ordered a classroom the more likely a teacher is to use group work, class discussion, role play and other less structured activities which are often interesting and highly motivating. The greater the order, the more opportunity there often is for creative freedom within that holding framework.

Considering the role of relationships mentioned in the last chapter, it is perhaps worth noting that an important part of handling relationships is the ability to recognise and manage one's own anger constructively and also to deal with anger from others. If unspoken and unacknowledged, anger can undermine relationships and can lead to inappropriate explosions of fury in which it is acted out unconsciously rather than being expressed verbally and more consciously. This chapter falls into four sections:

1. Power relations.   3. Anger and dealing with it.
2. Helping children manage conflict.   4. Minimising the incidence of conflict.

1. Power relations

An obvious example of an undesirable imbalance in power relations is that of bullying. Much has already been written on the subject. However, we would like to add a few points concerning those acting aggressively as a bully or in another way and those on the receiving end of aggression, verbal or otherwise, since understanding the power relationship involved may help teachers work with children when an aggressive incident has occurred. I use the terms 'victim' and 'aggressor' in inverted commas since they are roles people adopt at times in relation to each other or in their thinking about themselves, rather than static character traits. The following points outline some of the major features associated with aggressive and passive roles:

1. Someone adopting a bullying or aggressive role feels a 'victim' inside, that is to say, feels certain he or she has no choice in a particular situation or in some or many areas of his or her life.
2. The aggressive or bullying act is an attempt to induce in the 'victim' feelings similar to those experienced by the 'aggressor' but unacknowledged, for example fear, hopelessness, powerlessness.
3. There is a dynamic between 'victim' and 'aggressor', initiated and prescribed by the latter. This may be brief in the case of one instance of violence or verbal abuse, or ongoing, as in the case of bullying sustained over an extended period of time. The 'victim' is expected to behave in certain ways. (I am in no way suggesting that it is a 'victim's' fault if subject to an attack by an 'aggressor'; but that thinking in terms of a 'victim'–'aggressor' dynamic can provide a key for change in the future. This is not to deny that there are some incidents of usually very sudden and/or overwhelming aggression when little or nothing could be done.)
4. An aspect of the 'victim'–'aggressor' dynamic is that, if we experience being in a 'victim' position in one situation we often take on an 'aggressor' role later, treating someone else as a 'victim'. For example, if a child is shouted at during school, he or she may then shout or be rude or uncooperative later at home. If a teacher feels in a 'victim' position in relation to government policy, an OFSTED inspection, a head, part of the senior management staff, a colleague or parent, then he or she is more likely to adopt a more aggressive stance in relation to others, another adult, perhaps, or children. In other words, we tend to pass on the behaviour we receive, as we perceive it.
5. The 'victim'–'aggressor' dynamic is potentially very unstable since, at any time, the 'victim' can reverse roles, becoming an even fiercer 'aggressor' to a new 'victim', or can step outside the 'victim'–'aggressor' dynamic entirely. An example of this is found in the chidren's story book by Hans Wilhelm, *Tyrone the Horrible* (1989). The main character, Boland, has been bullied for some time

by the much bigger dinosaur, Tyrone. After several futile attempts to rebuff Tyrone which have been suggested by his friends, Boland finally hits on the way to change the dynamic between them. He makes sandwiches with a very hot and spicy filling so that, when Tyrone, next steals his sandwiches and eats them, he burns his mouth. Boland finally manages to do this because he suddenly realises he has the personal resources to do something about Tyrone, to stand up to him in some way, to speak out for himself and to show he cannot be intimidated.

6. A would-be 'aggressor' often picks on someone he or she finds different, difference being experienced as a threat.

Antidotes: ways out of the 'victim'–'aggressor' dynamic

A question of power
There are perhaps three possible ways of relating to others: you can adopt an aggressive role, trying to exert power over others; you can take on a very passive role, allowing others to exert power over you; or you can feel sufficiently confident of your power within to step outside the 'victim'–'aggressor' dynamic and focus on your own life and vision, aware of others but not involved in responding to them alone.

Although the *behaviour* of someone who takes on an 'aggressor' role is very different from that of someone adopting a 'victim' one, the root cause is fundamentally the same and may include a lack of belief in oneself, feelings of powerlessness, no awarenes of possible alternatives, a sense of having nothing to contribute, fear, lack of confidence, poor self-esteem, a lack of alternative social or communication skills or an inability to use them in a certain situation.

Strategies which help build confidence, self-esteem and a sense of inner power and purpose include:

- Any strategy which enables pupils to feel active participants in their learning, such as choosing, making decisions, taking responsibility. There are many examples throughout the book.
- Any strategy which helps pupils succeed.
- Praise.
- Positive interventions regarding behaviour (see the following chapter).
- Opportunities for making a contribution to others, for example, a project connected to improving the local environment or one contributing to the local community.
- Activities which are relevant, accessible and meaningful.
- Opportunities for developing and exercising initiative and creativity.
- Helping children feel respected, valued and special in some way.
- Work on accepting and valuing difference and diversity.
- An understanding of anger and aggression and techniques for managing anger.
- Opportunities for building rewarding relationships.

Alternative behaviour strategies
(i) Helping the 'aggressor'
Strategies similar to those outlined above can, over a period, help children develop confidence, self-esteem and a belief that they can make a difference, in other words,

that they have an inner strength they can direct constructively. In addition, it can be helpful to explore some of the different ways children could behave instead of fighting or intimidating others. One approach involves the adoption of:

- a body posture associated with relaxation and internal power;
- a role which captures the child's imagination, encapsulates desired behaviour and will have credibility among peers.

Techniques for helping children change behaviour are discussed in the following chapter.

(ii) Helping the 'victim'

Since the internal position of 'aggressor' and 'victim' are similar, even though the ways of expressing it are so diverse, the strategies for facilitating changes in behaviour can be the same. Any strategy which helps the child develop confidence, self-esteem and a belief he or she can make a difference can be of use. So can the adoption of a role, choosing someone real or fictional, or maybe even an animal as a model for standing, sitting, moving, breathing and behaving differently. Attention to body posture can be of considerable benefit in encouraging a child to try out more empowering behaviour: there will be a kind of body posture and thinking attached to a 'victim' role, an 'aggressor' role and one which is based on feeling confident and secure.

In addition to supporting a child in adopting a helpful role, it might also be fruitful to consider how he or she might respond if a friend behaved as the aggressor had done. Since there is a different dynamic between friends, the child is often able to find an effective response to counter an affront or an attack from a friend without difficulty. Knowing this can boost his or her confidence considerably. Frequently, children will think of very apt ways of dealing with situations once they are in touch with their own sense of power and are not involved directly in the troubling and intimidating dynamic which has been established.

A further approach is to explore how he or she is *expected* to behave by the 'aggressor' and then consider behaviour that would be very different from that. Usually this incorporates a relaxed, more expansive body posture. If a pupil loses momentum and returns to feeling powerless and responding in ways the 'aggressor' expects, then getting back into this posture can often help recapture the more positive outlook.

Talking not fighting

The following example illustrates how even five-year-olds can avoid fighting if they possess adequate communication skills and sufficient self-esteem, confidence and sense of their own personal power to apply them. This conversation also shows how a would-be 'aggressor' fails to be aggressive if the other refuses the 'victim' role and will not respond as expected. The girl, S, had invited the boy, D, home to play after school. When they arrived, however, S started pushing D around. He complained loudly and S's mother intervened. S went upstairs to see her father while D started investigating the toys. When S returned she picked up a rubber snake and began trying to push it down the back of D's jumper. The scene proceeded as follows:

Boy: 'Don't!' This was repeated on several occasions as he moved away and continued to play with a toy.

Girl: Chasing after him with the snake, 'It's poisonous and it's just touched you. You're dead now.'

Boy: 'No I'm not. I'm, wearing a suit of armour.'

Girl: 'No you're not.'

Boy: 'Yes I am. It's invisible.'

Girl: 'I can't see it.'

Boy: 'It's invisible.'

Girl: 'Where's your skin?'

Boy: 'Underneath.'

Girl: Going to get a toy frog to help the snake chase the boy. 'You're the Baddie and I'm the Goodie and I'm going to kill you.'

Boy: Avoiding the snake and frog, 'You shouldn't do this. I'm your guest. When you come to my house, I'm going to make you the Baddie then.'

Girl: Stepping back, 'It wasn't me, it was them' [the frog and snake]. She put the toys down, went over to where D was standing by the toy box, picked out a toy and both children started looking at it together and talking about it.

D avoided the 'victim' role in several ways and was able to do so only because of the sophisticated communication skills both children possessed. Firstly, he ignored the snake and carried on playing. Once S increased the pressure by saying the snake was poisonous and he was dead, D resorted to a fantasy protection: he was safe from her attacks. Then, when the frog was involved too and he was cast as the Baddie, he used reason, pointing out that guests should not be treated in this way and that she could expect the same treatment when visiting him. This reminder that her behaviour would have unpleasant consequences gave S a choice: she quickly chose to make peace and initiated another, cooperative activity.

During this interaction D remained confident of his own internal power throughout. It is easy to imagine how this could have been otherwise. He could easily have returned aggression with aggression at which point S would either have flipped into 'victim' role, or a possible fight would have ensued. If D had accepted 'victim' role and run away screaming and frightened, S would almost certainly have redoubled her efforts since he would have confirmed to her that her actions were indeed frightening. As it was, he indicated that he was not really threatened by her at all. Ignoring her did not work, however, since she wanted some acknowledgement of what she was doing. This he gave by the fantasy solution. Although he was not accepting the 'victim' role up to this point he had nevertheless been reacting to her provocation, parrying her assaults. When he told her she was not behaving properly towards a guest and would receive the same treatment, he was *taking charge and redefining the situation in his own terms.* She immediately complied. He had, however, given her a choice: that is to say, he did not disempower her, but left her the option of saving face. He also put a boundary on her behaviour by his last comments, adding a sense of safety to the situation. It is a tribute to the communication skills of both children that they managed to come to such an amicable resolution. It is also interesting that, four years later, they are very close friends.

This is an interesting exchange for several reasons. One of these is that it illustrates how well even very young children can manage conflict if they have the verbal skills with which to do so. If the boy, D, lacked these he would probably have hit or pushed S at some point to protect himself and any adult entering upon the scene would have been likely to tell him off for doing so. This is a fairly common pattern: a girl provokes a boy in some way, often verbally, and the boy responds physically or with greater force and gets blamed. Since girls often develop verbal skills earlier to a more sophisticated level than boys they can have an advantage in this area. If boys are given the skills with which to manage conflict verbally they have a choice: to respond physically, to parry insult with insult, words with words, or to come up with some other imaginative verbal response as in the example above. Many girls also require skills which can lead to a constructive outcome in managing conflict.

2. Helping children manage conflict

The need to deal with conflict

Feeling pressured by the demands of the curriculum, it is easy to disregard the need to equip children with the skills for resolving conflict. There are some compelling reasons, however, why it might be beneficial to do so.

1. When angry, children stop listening, stop concentrating and are unlikely to embark on creative work.
2. Disputes begun out of school or in the playground can often lead to disruptive behaviour in class. Considerable teacher time and effort can be subsequently involved in sorting out such incidents.
3. As mentioned earlier, without a sufficient level of emotional well-being, children cannot progress adequately. This is particularly relevant for those who have difficulty in sustaining friendships because they are frequently in conflict with others.
4. If children learn and practise the communication skills necessary for managing conflict creatively in primary school they will benefit hugely in secondary school and later in life. Projects carried out in America indicate that when children known for aggressive behaviour are equipped with alternative behaviour to fighting, including verbal skills, and learn how to recognise their own anger, the incidence of aggression declines steeply and achievement improves. Goleman (1996) cites one experimental programme at Duke University in which improvements were sustained into adolescence.

What children need in order to manage conflict creatively
- adequate self-esteem and confidence;
- skills in listening to others and in empathy;
- verbal skills;
- an awareness of non-aggressive body posture;
- an ethos which gives permission not to fight, that is to say, it is not 'sissy' to sort out quarrels without fighting;

- time to think, discuss and practise new behaviour;
- techniques to manage their own anger;
- alternative ways of 'proving' themselves and achieving; sometimes a new role may be helpful if a reputation of being 'tough' has given status before.

Without adequate skills children are more likely to resort to name-calling, teasing or violence if some disagreement arises. Although some pupils will have learnt such skills at home, many will not. Also there will be differences in approach stemming from a variety of cultural and other value systems. Consequently, it can be helpful if common strategies are worked out collaboratively before situations arise.

The 'what if?' game

This game could be played in an odd five minutes before a break. It is described in the section 'Offering skills and practice: introducing the idea of choice' in Chapter 5 (p. 125). Even though, in the heat of the moment, pupils may sometimes forget skills for resolving conflict peacefully, some will remember some of the time.

The peace table

Some basic negotiating skills involving listening, ways of developing empathy and joint problem-solving can be introduced to children and practised using the model of the peace table which is used in some schools and is described below.

This is a table where children go to sort out quarrels amongst themselves. At first a teacher, helper or parent goes with them to help them follow the instructions. After a while, children can go there without an adult. The children sit at the table either side of a corner or next to each other, in other words not opposite since enemies square up opposite each other and this position encourages conflict. Seating positions can thus help develop the idea that both children are, in fact, *on the same side with a common problem, the area of conflict lying between them.* Instructions for conducting the talk are written on card. In the example for infants (see Appendices), the cards are shaped like a goldfish and a budgie. Since many children may have difficulty reading, pictures can be added as a prompt.

3. Anger and managing it

Looking at anger

One of the difficulties with helping pupils manage conflict is the issue of anger. When angry, people tend to stop listening to others: as a participant on one of my workshops once said, 'Anger is a monologue'. Once you can begin listening to someone else again, the anger is starting to abate. Before this, however, it is easy to have ears for your own internal tape of grievances and indignation alone, often wanting to wallow in the feelings for a while. Some people like an audience at least at some point in order to hurt others or to let them know just how badly they have been treated.

Teachers are not therapists. It is not appropriate as a teacher to try to sort out a child's life or difficulties, even if that were possible. The teacher does, however, have responsibility for the smooth-running of the classroom and for helping children to learn, express themselves creatively and understand. At times the anger of one or more children may hinder their own progress and that of the class. It is not a question of indulging anger since children need to learn behaviour appropriate for different situations, but of helping children understand more about the process of anger and of equipping them with the skills to manage it in a variety of ways. Many will not know there are alternatives to hitting out, shouting or sulking and, unless they are aware of this and are given the skills, they can never have a choice.

Work on anger can be covered in a number of different topic areas. 'Myself', for example, could involve work on our emotions as well as our physical bodies. 'Our School' could consider the emotional life of the school: when children and teachers become angry, how they can deal with it, and so on. A topic such as 'The Victorians' could compare the lives of children living then and now, including attitudes towards anger and other emotions. Details of work would vary depending on the age of the children. Here are some ideas for adaptation.

The experience of anger

In dance or movement work children could be asked to move around the room in contrasting ways, taking care not to touch anyone else: happy, sad, calm, angry, frightened, confident, and so on. Angry movements might be big, noisy, tense. This could provide a starting point for discussing how we might appear to others when angry and how we feel. Another or additional approach is to ask pupils to stand or sit in an angry pose, either by copying how they have seen others sit and stand when angry or by adopting a pose familiar to them. Children are then asked to note for themselves how this feels, where they feel tense, how their breathing changes, and how their thinking is affected. Some children may start to *feel* angry during both these exercises so it is helpful to hold the posture for a few moments only while the children note their experience, then ask them to move, to stand if they had been seated, shake away the feeling, take a few deep breaths and then go floppy all over before sitting down gently. Then they can compare their experiences.

A particular value of these exercises can be that children become aware of the connection between how they sit, stand or move and how they feel and think. In other words, *they will not be able to stop feeling angry unless they move even a little, changing their body posture and breathing pattern.* If, through talking and listening they begin to feel less angry then they will naturally shift body posture as the anger ebbs away. Thus the emotions and thinking may trigger the change in body posture, or vice versa. The two are, however, inextricably linked. Often it is useful to begin change with the breathing and body posture since these are more tangible and facilitate listening and empathy. This link between mind and body is important if pupils wish to be able to change their behaviour in any way or to manage their anger and keep their temper.

Similarly in music, children could be asked to create different emotional atmospheres through the sounds they make. They can later discuss the kinds of sounds which characterise anger. The exercises with music and movement are likely to result in a number of adjectives which describe anger, for example, harsh, loud, sudden, big, strong, fierce. The children could continue the theme through art work and through writing poems.

'You make me angry' or 'I am angry with you'?

An interesting exercise is one in which children carry out a survey to assess what different people get angry at. The information can then be collated as a bar chart. The class decide on nine or ten things or people they and adults get angry at, for example, teachers telling them off, brothers or sisters, parents or carers not letting them do something, bosses, children talking loudly, difficult sums, dog mess on pavements and in parks, politicians, having to go to bed early, and so on. Some children collect the data, asking members of other classes, teachers, parents, carers and friends. Each person is allowed only one choice. Other children collect different information, this time asking what children and adults do not feel angry about on the same list. Again only one choice per person is allowed.

The result of this usually illustrates that people feel angry about different things and that some are not angry at all about the very thing others are most infuriated with. In other words, *we feel* angry in response to different stimuli: nothing makes us angry. This realisation is a useful first step in anyone taking responsibility for anger.

What can you do with anger?

The story-book *Angry Arthur* can serve as a starting point for considering what anger is and the consequences of expressing it. Does the boy in the book really destroy the universe with his anger? Or is it that he wants to destroy it or is he frightened that his anger might do so? Is it dangerous to feel angry? Does anger have positive or negative results? This question is a demanding one and there may be a range of views. Children are often punished for being angry, frequently because they act out the anger, rather than expressing it verbally and using it constructively. Older children can brainstorm examples of people starting out feeling angry about something, often injustice, and then using the energy involved to bring about positive change, for example, Florence Nightingale, William Wilberforce and others active in social reform.

When people are feeling angry they often have other emotions, too, masked by the anger, particularly fear or sadness. To take two minor examples:

- someone might be cross because of missing a bus, but underneath this he or she is anxious about the consequences of being late;
- another person is angry at losing a favourite book or article of clothing, but underneath is sad at the loss.

Some people find it easier to be aware of and to express anger than sadness or fear. For others sadness comes to the fore, and for yet others fear. Pupils can make stylised masks representing the three emotions of anger, sadness and fear in the style of Greek drama. They can be made so that all three can be worn at once, emphasising the point that very often all three emotions are present with only one visible.

Anger can become a habit, especially if children are unaware that other behaviour is possible, lack the skills to behave differently, and/or if it has been effective in some way in the past. Maybe it gained them attention, even if it was negative attention, maybe it helped them get their way. Sometimes it can be helpful to consider the range of how different people deal with anger and which options are most likely to result in pleasant consequences. This provides pupils with the information that it is possible to behave differently. Understanding this is essential if children wish to manage their anger in a new way.

As a whole class or in groups pupils can offer suggestions of what people can do when they are angry. The teacher could write this on the board. Another way of considering this material is for the teacher to give small groups of pupils a list of behaviours. These could include shouting, hitting, walking off angrily and slamming the door, throwing things, saying, 'I'm angry!', keeping your temper and talking to the person concerned later on when you have calmed down a little, keeping your temper and talking about it later to someone else. Groups then have to decide what are the most likely consequences of each behaviour in each of three scenarios, for example:

- two pupils from different classes are angry with each other in the playground, one called the other a name and he or she responded in kind;
- two friends are cross with each other in class because one thinks the other was responsible for losing his or her toy and the other is angry for being wrongly accused;
- a pupil has been told off by a teacher for something he or she did not do.

Following on from this, older pupils could write imaginative stories involving someone angry or could describe real incidents. They could then write alternative endings: one in which a character dealt with his or her anger destructively by acting it out in some way, and one in which anger was handled more constructively. The aim would be to illustrate the fact that a destructive result to anger is not inevitable. Another way of approaching this theme would be to read a passage or story which involved a character getting angry. Leaving the passage unfinished, ask the class to write endings to the scene.

These exercises lead to the point that feeling angry is one thing, the responsibility lies in *choosing* what to do with it. In order to be able to choose rather than being swept along on the wave of emotion to repeat old patterns of behaviour it is necessary to be able to create a gap between getting angry and acting. In other words, it is essential to be able to keep your temper long enough to think of the consequences of a hasty response. Another way of seeing it is creating a cooling off period, whether this is a brief gap between feeling the emotion and acting (as in the old advice of counting to ten) or a longer period for reflection. Some schools, classrooms and playgrounds have a calm corner or a quiet place where children can go when they feel angry in order to calm down. This can be very useful for those children who are used to reacting quickly and aggressively to perceived provocation. If they can learn to walk away from a situation to a safe place where they can calm down then this is one way of beginning to keep their temper.

Another way is to help pupils create a brief gap between feeling anger and acting, a gap in which they can develop an internal quiet place from which to choose what to do. The advice of counting to ten has some value since it provides a gap and redirects the mind to attend to something else, namely counting. This technique might work for some. It can perhaps be refined by encouraging children to breathe out three times while stepping to the side and feeling floppy all over before counting to ten. As we saw above, it is impossible to remain feeling angry when the body posture and breathing pattern connected to it are relaxed. (For greater detail on how to create a gap in which to choose a different kind of behaviour, see the section 'Offering skills and practice: introducing the idea of choice' in Chapter 5.)

If children have practised developing an internal quiet place as described below, they may find this helpful to imagine for a few seconds before deciding what to do: walk away, tell someone, hit the person they are angry with, start fighting, shout, and so on. This technique can be practised in PE or dance, the children standing in an angry posture and then moving out of it. It could also be rehearsed in the 'What if' game mentioned earlier.

An internal quiet place

Helping children develop an internal quiet place can bring many benefits in addition to its use in dealing with anger. There are many ways of encouraging development of this internal calm. Here is one of them. The exercise can be usefully preceded by looking at pictures of beautiful places or by listening to some peaceful music.

The children sit in a relaxed position with their eyes closed and imagine a beautiful place usually outdoors. It might be in a garden, a park, a wood, a field, by a river, by the school pond, by the sea, by a waterfall, in the sky, in space among the stars. Tell them there is no right or wrong in this exercise. The idea is to close their eyes and experiment. It does not need to be a large or grand place; it could be the sense of sitting under the tree in the playground, or looking at just one flower or listening to birdsong. It can be in sunshine, rain or snow. The children can conjure up their quiet place in any way they like: seeing it, hearing the sounds associated with it, feeling they are in it, smelling and sensing everything around. The important thing is that the children enjoy visiting this place, feel calm and safe there and are refreshed and supported by it. In a sense you are asking the children to develop their own internet by using their imagination: in seconds they have the power to transport themselves anywhere they like. It is helpful if the teacher sits quietly too, thinking of something calming while the children are involved in this exercise.

When it is time to finish, ask the children to imagine saying goodbye silently to their special place, before finding a way of getting back quickly to it. This might be by shrinking it and filing it away in an imaginary computer in their heads or popping it into a pocket over their heart for safe keeping, or it might be by saying to themselves a special word or by turning a key or pressing a button that transports them instantly from there to the present and vice versa. The important thing is that they have a means of moving between the classroom and their quiet place with ease and that they bring their sense of calm back with them.

Initially some children might find this exercise difficult, but it is simply a question of practice. The first session might last a few minutes, after which some children might like to share their experience. Once they are used to it, children can usually access their quiet place easily. Visiting it frequently for very brief periods, maybe just one minute, is most useful since children are then more likely to develop the skills and habit of using it themselves. It can be used in many ways, such as at the beginning or end of the day, to change the atmosphere in the classroom, to give children a break between activities, as well as in dealing with anger. It helps children in learning to sit still and quietly, in developing confidence in their imagination and in exploring which sensory channel is most useful for them.

A calm corner

The calm corner is best designed to represent the opposite of anger, that is to say, it is quiet and still, with some large cushions for sitting on if possible, and, perhaps, some drapes in pastel colours. There may be some beautiful, peaceful pictures, a tape player with calming music, paper and crayons for drawing, plasticine for modelling and books to read. It could be the reading corner with an additional use. In the playground, there could be some seats and plants, maybe some books supplied in dry weather or if the area is under cover. It could be a place children go to talk quietly or to be reflective at playtimes, as well as when seeking to calm down.

One boy in Year 2, F, was referred to me because he was having frequent outbursts of anger in which he destroyed his work before storming from the class. Other pupils were upset by this and the teacher was understandably concerned. She had spoken to the parents who were aware of this pattern of behaviour which seemed to erupt from time to time when F was feeling insecure. The family had recently moved house and F had found the change unsettling, especially since he had left a close friend who had lived next door. His parents agreed to talk more to F about the loss of moving from the house he had lived in all his life and from leaving his friend. They would also set up some visits so the friends could meet up. F did not appear to have any particular difficulty with school work.

Rather than working with him individually, we decided to include anger in the topic for the whole class. The teacher created a calm corner in the room so that F could go there to calm down if he needed. Over the following weeks the teacher incorporated work on anger into the topic as outlined above. F's behaviour calmed down relatively quickly so that the frequency of outbursts was reduced from two or three a day to that many a week. The number of visits he made to the calm corner gradually reduced over the term. By the end of term he rarely went there.

All this might have occurred naturally as a result of him settling into his new home and feeling reassured about maintaining contact with a good friend. However, we thought that the process of adaptation had probably been accelerated and that the anger work had provided him with a useful model and some skills to deal with his anger on the next occasion that he felt insecure. In particular, it had given him permission to feel angry while reminding him of the responsibility he had in dealing with it. The fact that he was allowed to go to the calm corner emphasised the point that he could feel angry as long as he dealt with it sensibly. He had been provided with suggestions for alternative behaviour and had learnt that he became angry rather than others made him so. He had also developed some skills for keeping his temper.

Some additional points about anger

1. There are differing cultural and religious views concerning anger.
2. Teachers can also feel very angry at times too. Some of the techniques outlined in this section can be useful at any age.
3. Anger is a response to a real or imagined attack of some kind or to frustration, real or imagined, of a desire or need. The attack may be physical or emotional. Adrenalin floods through the body providing it with extra energy to fight, flee, shout or grab, etc.
4. If there is a reason for anger in the past which is unresolved and remains simmering at some level, then another incident which is a reminder of that original situation is likely to be met with additional anger. In the present this may well appear to be an overreaction.
5. Many people find that talking about their anger to someone who is sympathetic can be extremely helpful, since in explaining to someone who will listen it is often possible to become clearer about the issues involved and the real source of anger.
6. Many people also find that some safe physical exercise helps them dissipate some of the tension from anger and to feel calmer. After dispelling some of the anger tension in the body 'centring' can help return us to a state of calm. This concept is explained in the next chapter in the section 'The power of thinking'.
7. Most people will probably want their anger acknowledged. As a teacher it is often helpful to acknowledge and contain anger, not indulge it. If someone who is angry is ignored he or she may well act in an increasingly angry manner, for a while at least.
8. The following measures can help reduce anger in the long and short term.
    *   Techniques for releasing anger tension in the body safely and calming down: this may include various kinds of exercise, running, swimming, football, hitting a punch-bag, dancing.
    *   A supportive, calming environment which provides the opportunity to relax and get involved in doing something else to divert attention from the anger.
    *   Emotional support: someone to talk to.
    *   Doing something creative since anger is often associated with feelings of powerlessness. This can be anything, such as mending a bike, tidying a room, making people laugh, drawing a picture, deciding what you will do or say in a situation.
    *   Communication skills which make it easier to express anger verbally, when appropriate, rather than acting angrily.

- The more long-term task of building self-esteem so that confidence for dealing with situations increases and less incidents are considered to be threats or attacks. Consequently, the potential number of angry responses decreases. Learning to stand and move in a relaxed way can also help in this.

4. Minimising the incidence of conflict

Conflict will always occur to some degree or another and if pupils are equipped with skills for resolving it constructively it can become an area for development and learning. However, it is reasonable to try to find ways of minimising the number and severity of incidents. Strategies which can reduce the incidence of conflict include:

- developing a whole-school policy on managing conflict constructively;
- employing management strategies which minimise the likelihood of disputes arising, for example, orderly ways of coming into school from the playground and hanging up coats, norms for moving around the building and the classroom, seating plans, rotas for helpers;
- developing the techniques discussed earlier in this chapter for helping children understand and manage anger, learn communication skills and practise ways of resolving conflict;
- considering playtimes as a major source of potential conflict and developing strategies for helping children play constructively.

Constructive playtimes

Common scenarios
For many children playtimes are unhappy times. Much of the bullying there is occurs during breaks, arguments develop, children wander without playmates hoping no one will notice they have no friends. Some children frequently get into trouble at these times and this can contribute to their disaffection with school. Teachers often have to deal with aggressive incidents of one kind or another which started during breaks. There are several reasons for this, including the fact that:

- Many playgrounds are dismal areas of tarmac with little that can lend itself to playing.
- The children who are most likely to become involved in creating conflict or in carrying out some aggressive act are those least able to manage the unstructured, less supervised time at breaks. On the whole, they are the least able to initiate games themselves and may well lack the communication skills to ask to join another game in a way likely to be accepted. They often lack the collaborative skills needed to play together.
- There may well also be groups of older juniors who are bored, too 'cool' to play and who want to spend their time in more inaccessible parts of the school or toilets talking, possibly intimidating younger children just by their presence and maybe getting up to other kinds of mischief.

Possible projects

If playtimes were more assuredly positive experiences for more children this could greatly help with motivation: for some children this might tip the balance, giving them a real reason to come to school. For example, if the boy in Chapter 1 given 500 lines for playing football were instead able to practise his skill even once a week in playtimes his attitude towards the institution as a whole might be improved.

The individual teacher obviously has less control over what happens in the playground than in the classroom but, nevertheless, may make some suggestions in staff meetings or through the PTA. At the very least, he or she could put the issue of playtimes on the agenda. Possible conflict might be reduced if there are more activities the children might like to get involved in, if there is more supervision and if there is a specific code of practice for the playground with clear sanctions everyone knows. Unfortunately, there is usually the perennial problem of insufficient funds either to reconstruct the playground as an exciting and stimulating environment or to employ more lunch time staff. However, the following suggestions often require only some initial organisation and little money.

1. There are several ways in which the children can be involved in creating a more interesting playground in which conflict is less likely. For example:
   - drawing up the code of practice, including sanctions, for playground behaviour;
   - giving suggestions as to how playtimes could be improved and what activities they would like;
   - with a clear brief, older children can supervise the activities of younger children; in one school, for example, Year 6 pupils choose the teams and act as referees when other years play football.
2. Different areas of the playground can be designated for specific activities, leaving some space for children who wish to play creatively on their own. The activities might include chalk drawing, chess or draughts played with large pieces, a quiet area with books, skipping, a patball area, netball or baseball hoops and, if space allows, cricket, rounders and football.
3. Some schools have particular 'seasons' when certain activities are allowed for a term or half term, each governed by its own set of rules. The school year starts, for example, with the conker season when children can bring in conkers to play with and admire. They are allowed a maximum of ten each and must keep them during work time in a named bag in a special box in the classroom. As described in Chapter 2, other seasons include marbles, skipping, hopscotch and patball.
4. Making links with the local community can be very fruitful in at least two ways.
   - It might provide a source of people willing to supervise lunch time activities on a voluntary basis, for example, sixth formers from a local secondary school, some people who are retired or unemployed or those who work locally. (Adults working with pupils in schools will, of course, always be expected to undergo a police check as a standard procedure.)
   - Some parents, carers or members of the local community might be willing to offer a specific activity or club depending on their interests and expertise, for example, starting a school magazine produced by the pupils with adult supervision, a science club, a gardening club, an art club, a film or book club.

Making links with the local community can sometimes lead to the children being able to use time during playtimes to contribute to people in the area, giving a concert, perhaps, or doing artwork to be displayed locally.

This chapter has dealt with:

Power relations

- Antidotes: ways out of the 'victim–'aggressor' dynamic

Helping children manage conflict

- The need to deal with conflict
- The 'what if?' game
- The peace table

Anger and managing it

- Looking at anger
- The experience of anger
- 'You make me angry' or 'I am angry with you'?
- What can you do with anger?
- An internal quiet place
- A calm corner
- Some additional points about anger

Minimising the incidence of conflict

- Constructive playtimes.

Chapter 5

Managing troublesome behaviour

> Within each of us there is a place that provides the nurturing and support we
> need in order to grow, and make decisions, to give and receive love. It is the
> home of our intuition. I call it the quiet place. It is the place which supports all,
> knows all, but is attached to nothing.
>
> (Kaleghl Quinn, Stand your Ground, 1983)

1. Juggling

Part of the difficulty in dealing with the troublesome behaviour of one child is the
fact that you have the rest of the class to teach! This results in the sensation that,
very often, you are expected to juggle with an ever increasing number of balls. As
one experienced teacher, Susan House, writes:

> All the pupils in my Year 3 class are lovely children individually. Together,
> however, they presented me with a real challenge. This is largely because of the
> wide ability range and the fact that there are very few children working more
> independently at level 2A and 2B: there is a group of five at level 3 who work
> very quickly and are eager to forge ahead, a large group working at level 2C who
> need considerable support, one pupil at stage 2 special needs and two at stage 3.
> The latter receive half an hour a week each special needs teaching out of the
> classroom. A classroom assistant is available to work with the class for three
> hours a week. One problem is that, particularly at the beginning of the year,
> most of the class lacked the confidence to work independently, especially during
> the literacy hour and in maths. If I gave special attention to the children working
> at higher levels at these times, squabbles and fighting soon erupted in the rest of
> the class. Consequently, I could really do this only when the classroom assistant
> or a parent was available to work with one group.
>
> It is in this context that Y's behaviour caused me particular concern. He is at
> stage 3 special needs and joined the class from a parallel group on coming into
> the juniors. In class he sucked his knuckles all the time, quietly fidgeted in his
> seat, punched other children and periodically threw things. In the playground he
> often punched other children and did not join in games with the others. One
> disturbing thing about him when he came into the class was that he did not

smile and it was difficult to make eye contact with him. He appeared, at seven years of age, quite 'vacant', disinterested in what was going on around him, with no friends. He smiled for the first time only six weeks into the term. His body posture and behaviour suggested to me that he was unhappy, frightened, angry and felt completely alone and inadequate. It was as if he was in such a nervous state of panic that he could not think clearly. He did not seem to have a learning difficulty as such: his learning seemed to be delayed because of his frozen emotional state. Consequently, he began the year working at the level of pupils in Reception. He had been able to do more at the end of last year in the infants when his behaviour had been more acceptable. The change of class had clearly put him back, possibly replicating some of the trauma he had experienced out of school: his grandfather who was living with the family died; his mother died; the family was split up, his two half-sisters and his half-brother going to live with an aunt. Y remained in the now empty house with his father who has subsequently remarried.

My aim for the first half term was to build up trust and to help Y feel more comfortable in the class by succeeding in work and managing to keep his behaviour more appropriate. He clearly could not learn much until he felt less frightened and more confident. Only then, too, would he be likely to stop hitting others and throwing things. My difficulty was finding things Y could manage to do, bearing in mind the needs of the rest of the class, in order to praise him. I devised special tasks for him. These included drawing, building with blocks, building with Lego, matching colours and shapes, throwing dice and counting blocks, a simple bingo game he played with a classmate. I organised a rota of parents to read to him for 15 minutes every morning. I also started to build up a relationship with his stepmother who wanted to be supportive, but was not sure how she could help. After a few weeks, however, she bought Y a desk at home. He was very proud of this and would sometimes do drawings I had asked him to do at home. He took the bingo and other games home to play with his father or stepmother.

By two weeks after half term Y had settled in well. He had made friends with a couple of boys in the class and seemed much happier. He still required considerable input but was able to manage the work I was setting and was gaining in confidence. I was also feeling more confident in dealing with him! After Christmas his cousin came into the class on work experience. She is 15, very capable and keen to work both with Y and others. This has strengthened links with his father and stepmother and delighted Y, as he has someone of his own in class.

The most troublesome behaviour in the class now came from four boys working at level 2C. They demanded a lot of my time and when I was busy with other members of the class would instantly start arguing, annoying each other or fighting. I had placed them on a table together so that I could easily work with them as a group, but this strategy was clearly not working. I split them up, each sitting next to pupils who could work more independently. I would call them to my desk to explain and discuss work and then they would go back to their seats to do it. After a while this seemed to help, although they remained very needy.

The other group which continued to cause me concern were the children who worked at a higher level. During maths and literacy times they always finished their work quickly and I did not feel confident that I was stretching them sufficiently. Although they did not misbehave as such, they were very demanding since they were eager to work and I found it difficult to meet their needs along with everyone else in the class. I devised a number of enjoyable activities so that they could choose what to do. These included drawing a story board of a book we have read together during literacy hour, making a small book, particularly with flaps, pop-ups, etc., about our topic or something of their own choice, activities connected to current crazes, for example, designing a yo-yo, making their own version of Pokémon cards. They also had their class readers. This system seemed to take the pressure off me as I had hoped.

However, I felt less effective when the class was working as a whole than I had earlier in the term and there seemed to be a general sense of unease and nerviness. When sitting on the mat the children shuffled a lot, annoying neighbours by prodding them, pulling their hair, and so on. There was also a considerable amount of calling out, often relevant, but nonetheless disruptive. As a result, times of giving instructions and whole-class discussions took longer than need be and I constantly had to remind pupils to put up their hands, sit still and listen. This change might have been partly due to tensions following an unfavourable OFSTED in the school and a change of senior management. There was considerable demoralisation, anxiety and upheaval, plans were often changed at the last minute and lessons interrupted. Amidst all this I sometimes found it difficult to remain calm and focused, so it is not surprising the children were also affected. Thinking about it for a while I decided to do the following.

- I revisited the class behaviour code. We had discussed this at the beginning of term, but now I asked the pupils to think how they could help each other learn and enjoy school. We drew up a list which included, 'Keep your hands and feet to yourself', 'Put your hand up to answer' and 'Listen to anyone speaking to the whole class'. We pinned the code up around the classroom and when someone breached it, instead of telling them to behave as appropriate, I could just say their name and point to the relevant part of the code. This at least saved me from appearing to nag the children and they seemed to take more responsibility for themselves.
- We start the day on the carpet for literacy. Those who sit appropriately, showing they are ready to work, are invited to sit on a chair. They love this! Only 4 or 5 children are allowed to sit on a chair for that lesson. Chairs are in a semi-circle at the back.
- I praised the children whenever possible for being a cooperative and helpful class and for working well together. I have found lots of praise and encouragement work, but only if it is genuine: the children know if it is not merited. I had been concerned that telling them off frequently for the endless niggles and interruptions was giving them the impression that they were a 'naughty' class. I wanted them to feel proud of belonging to the class and to believe they could work well together and help one another. I was careful to

use a positive commands like 'Sit properly' or 'Stand still', rather than 'Don't fidget' or 'You're not lining up sensibly' which can sound like nagging. I also praised good behaviour which others would emulate, for example, 'Mark is lining up sensibly. Well done, Mark!' instead of 'Mary, don't poke Jane'.

- I included collaborative activities whenever possible, trying to structure them carefully so it was easy for the groups to work successfuly. In dance, for example, I asked them in three's and four's to make up a dance to go with some music we had listened to in class. They did this extrememly well. Our topic was Invaders and Settlers so I had groups working together to paint some maps on cardboard illustrating the Romans invading Britain by sea.
- I set up a new system to minimise the calling out and this worked beautifully with the worst offenders. The children receive three warnings which means they are allowed to interrupt three times. However, on the fourth interruption they forfeit their entitlement to a red sticker. It is not necessary to raise my voice. Sometimes I say quietly, 'Joe, that is the second time you've called out . . .'. As I have at least four children who were causing problems calling out this has been a life-saver. I do try to set realistic targets. I want them to be able to achieve their sticker.
- We often sit quietly without talking or fidgeting for 30 seconds or a minute before we actually begin to work. This is long enough to calm the class, but it is not demanding the impossible.
- I emphasised the rewards they could gain for excellent work, thoughtfulness to others, following the class guidelines, and so on, and gave them out whenever possible. Rewards could be earnt individually, as a class, or a child could earn one for the whole class. They included stickers for their individual commendation books, an extra story on the carpet, or choices on Friday afternoon when work is finished, for example, a joke session, playing with Lego, showing magic tricks, doing drama or watching a video.
- I tried to improve the environment in the classroom so as to make it feel more separate from the upheaval and tension in the rest of the school. I brought in some plants to make it look a bit different and started to play a tape of calming music as the children came into class at the beginning of the day.
- I tried to stay calmer myself. I realised that although I was expecting the children to sit still and concentrate I rarely did this myself. So I made a point of sitting quietly and focusing on just one thing for 10 or 15 minutes every day. I also listened to calming music when preparing for the day, sometimes at lunch time and when tidying up.

I certainly felt more in charge after doing all this and the children did seem to settle down, apart from beginning to get excited by the prospect of Christmas and its activities. Two boys who had been working at level 2C and causing some disruption have recently come on leaps and bounds. For one of them, the difference came when I made a direct link with his mother. I decided I was going to say something nice to her about him whenever I saw her. His behaviour had not improved at all, so I said things like, 'We're still working on behaviour but there's been a big improvement in the quality of his work'. I had to do this on at least four occasions before she gave me eye contact. Up till then I think she was feeling so embarrassed and helpless regarding her son that she had avoided me whenever possible in case I had something else unpleasant to say about him. Once she realised he could do good work and she felt better about things his behaviour started to improve.

I have noticed with parents in the past that it is more useful to say something nice about their child as well as any criticism I want to make. This gives balance and seems to help everyone. Having pointed out to a parent, with the child present, what we're working on together to improve, I can then refer back to this if the child seems to need help. For example, something like, 'When your mum comes in tonight she's going to expect some good work. Why don't you come and sit here and get that finished. Then you can feel really proud when she's here and you show it to her.'

It has not been easy this year, but at least now the children have begun to feel like my class.

2. Troublesome behaviour

What is a teacher's role?

Most children can manage to adapt to the system of discipline and order set up by a school. Some, those who are most insecure and least confident, find it harder to meet demands and may express this through rude, aggressive or disruptive behaviour of one kind or another. For these children, the teacher usually has to be extremely resourceful in adapting the system to some degree in order to better meet their needs.

In working with a child's unwanted behaviour, a teacher's aim is to:

- re-establish or maintain a calm, purposeful and comfortable working environment for *all* pupils.

With the individual child a teacher's aim is to:

- build confidence and self-esteem;
- build a trusting relationship;
- adapt the environment and activities so that the pupil is less likely to resort to unwanted behaviour;
- maintain boundaries firmly and kindly, diverting the pupil gently and persistently from unwanted to alternative, desirable behaviour, helping him or her develop behaviour which is appropriate in the classroom and playground;
- facilitate cooperative working partnerships and friendships with peers;
- motivate and inspire;
- enable him or her to learn, think and understand.

Since a teacher is neither therapist nor social worker it is not appropriate to probe into personal difficulties a pupil may have. A teacher's role is to teach and to help a child develop the confidence, skills and understanding which will be useful in life, whatever difficulties he or she encounters outside school. A working understanding of a pupil's behaviour can often be helpful in this since it may suggest ways of managing him or her effectively so that he or she can at least cope, at best succeed in school.

Getting an understanding

Behaviour is generally perceived as troublesome when it disrupts the teacher's plans, upsets other class members, or in some way disturbs the process of teaching and learning in the classroom. In other words, the behaviour is *inappropriate* in the context of the classroom and is unacceptable since it detracts from the education of the other pupils. The question remains of how to deal with such behaviour and the children exhibiting it and, above all, how to encourage desirable behaviour. General prevention techniques are discussed in earlier chapters. This section focuses on managing the individual in a way which is, in the long term, likely to produce least disruption and will most help the child develop more acceptable behaviour.

It is possible to trace a line of cause and effect: if a human being is in difficulty he or she will frequently create difficulties for others as well as for him or herself. If a child in your class habitually causes you problems, he or she is not the problem (even though it may feel like this), he or she *has* a problem. This difference in perception can of itself alter your way of handling a situation and, therefore, the outcome.

Some children are simply too sad, too anxious or too angry to learn. Indeed, as we saw in Chapter 3, the three emotions are often all present and one or other may come to the surface unexpectedly. Thus a pupil who is anxious or sad may suddenly become very angry. Anger may be easier to feel than sadness or fear.

Some children may simply be very bored by school and, consequently, any disruptive behaviour they exhibit is understandable since they are expressing their discomfort at being in such a situation. Others may feel that they are failures and that school has little to offer them. This is likely to be particularly true of pupils with learning difficulties and those whose primary representational system is kinaesthetic and who learn by doing and feeling rather than by seeing and hearing. In Gardner's model of Multiple Intelligences, it is those children who do not have strengths in the areas of linguistic and mathematical logical intelligence who are likely to rebel against a programme which is often targeted at certain skills and abilities: reading, writing and numeracy skills.

Disruptive or reasonable?

It could be said that all behaviour is 'reasonable' if seen from the particular point of view of the person responsible for it. That is to say, behaviour that is totally unreasonable in a classroom could be said to be 'reasonable' if seen from the child's position, even if it could never be permitted. I am not suggesting that disruptive behaviour should be sanctioned. Far from it. The point I am making is that *understanding the thinking behind undesirable behaviour may provide a key for relating to the child in such a way that he or she is more likely to adopt acceptable behaviour in the future.* Rather than assuming that the child is determined to make your life as difficult as possible and is simply bad, it can be useful to ask *why* he or she is resorting to disruptive behaviour: habit, lack of alternative skills, preferring to disrupt than appear stupid, frustration at not being able to do the work, attempts to gain peer approval because of poor self-esteem, the need to feel 'powerful' in some way, as a protest against authority, out of a desire for attention, out of boredom or a sense of not being involved, as mentioned above, or for a specific reason, as with the girl with the scraps of paper referred to in Chapter 1.

It is often useful to consider what the behaviour might be saying or showing. It is unlikely to be random and will be communicating something about and doing something for the pupil. It may, perhaps, illustrate and confirm his or her world view or perceived position in it. Thus it will in some way help the pupil make sense of the world. It may be a deeply entrenched belief resulting from earlier experiences or may have been triggered by a specific incident. Sometimes it is almost as if the pupil has a particular script of a play illustrating his or her stance in life. The undesirable behaviour is the cue for the teacher to respond in a way the child expects according to that script. If the teacher does so, the child's self-image is confirmed. The self-image is usually a troublesome one or else the behaviour would not be regularly disruptive. If the teacher follows the script offered and confirms the pupil's self-image and world view the undesirable behaviour has been successful and has been reinforced.

Thus if a child views him or herself as a nuisance, his or her behaviour is likely to reflect this in some way and will probably be extremely annoying, provoking the teacher to call him or her a nuisance. This was certainly my experience in dealing with a boy in Year 7, W, about whom I had heard many complaints before our first meeting. Three teachers and the head teacher related to me aspects of his undesirable behaviour and how it affected them and the class. His disruptive behaviour invariably led to some kind of conflict with the teacher. In addition, he frequently became involved in fights with peers. I noticed that, quite independently, in talking about him all four of them said at one time or another, 'He's impossible'. This alerted me to a possible script along these lines, that W's deep belief about himself was that he was unmanageable, 'impossible'. Since one of W's difficulties was relating to peers, it was agreed that I should do a structured activity with him and two classmates in the library so that he would have the opportunity of building working relationships that could be transferred to the classroom. Sure enough, within half an hour of my working with them I heard myself say, to my own astonishment and horror, 'W, you're impossible!' Usually I am careful not to interpret behaviour in this way. In addition, I had been previously alerted to his behaviour and the response he tried to provoke from teachers. In spite of this, I had swallowed his script whole within a very short space of time and had confirmed his world view instantly: his belief about himself was very powerful and his behaviour was equally convincing!

Taking the role offered and helping to confirm the child's self-image reinforces the disruptive or angry behaviour. It is, in a way, also 'safe' since it confirms the pupil's world view and challenges nothing. However, the child's strategy for making sense of the world is in itself destructive since it gets in the way of learning and leads to conflict. The pupil may also continue with increasingly extravagent behaviour until a limit is set.

In gaining an understanding of the child's behaviour and possible script, it is often helpful to observe him or her carefully and, when away from the class, to:

- Consider dispassionately the child's behaviour: what is it saying; how does it appear to an uninvolved observer? Behaviour is often quite literal. What does it do for the child?
- Is there a pattern to the behaviour? What triggers it?
- Ask yourself how *you* feel on the other end of the behaviour.
- Try out the pupil's body posture for a few minutes to feel what it is like in his or her shoes. How does he or she sit, stand, walk? From this position, how does the world look? How would you regard learning, school, authority figures in general and teachers in particular? How comfortable do you feel? How confident? How would a teacher's instruction or reprimand sound from here?

Once you can see a pattern of behaviour and can get an idea of how it might feel from the child's position, it is often easier to find strategies to deal with the behaviour a little more satisfactorily. At the very least you may feel better about it. Very often the pupil's behaviour is such that the teacher ends up feeling how they feel. For example, if a child feels angry, frustrated, powerless, his or her behaviour may be such that the teacher ends up feeling angry, frustrated or powerless in response. Understanding this can often provide the key to managing the behaviour more effectively, sometimes by refusing the role offered in the script.

An alternative approach which does not confirm the self-image, consistently maintains firm boundaries and which presents the child with alternative ways of viewing him or herself may be of use. Also, a balance must always be struck between the smooth running of activities for the rest of the class and the needs of an individual. A teacher's aim is to facilitate the learning and educational development of *all* children in the class. Sometimes introducing an alternative self-image for a pupil helps in achieving this.

A different approach: offering a new self-image

B started school in January. He had not attended nursery before joining reception and found it hard to fit in. His concentration span was very short and he fidgeted wildly, sprawling back on his chair and bumping into and leaning on other children on the mat. He had missed a lot of preschool stimulation and conversation and did not know, for example, the names of colours. He frequently hit his classmates who were soon frightened of him. In the playground he stood watching the other children without making any attempts to join in or talk to them. At the end of the first two weeks, he had been labelled the 'naughty boy' of the class by the other children who avoided him. The teacher and assistants also dealt with him with a certain apprehension. Thinking about his behaviour, it suggested that he was very frightened by finding himself in such new surroundings and that he perceived himself as being totally unacceptable, an outsider who could not fit in. He was also consistently failing to live up to the school's expectations regarding work and behaviour.

His class teacher had a choice:

1. To respond to him by following the script he seemed to be offering, telling him off, blaming him, isolating him from the rest of the class and generally confirming him in his self-image;

2. Gradually to change his self-image by treating him differently. This would entail strategies which would help him feel less alienated and frightened and would make it easier for him to succeed than to fail. It would be made clear that hitting and disturbing other children were unacceptable and he would be helped to develop alternative behaviour.

In the short term, the first option seemed very easy to do since his behaviour was inviting rejection: his script seemed to be that he was 'naughty' and did not fit in, the teacher being pushed by his behaviour to exclude him from joint activities and the group. It would have been easy to reject him as the 'problem' in the class. The teacher, however, embarked upon the more long-term strategy of option number two. She immediately devised a number of measures to help build his confidence and change his view of himself.

- She asked B where he would find it easiest to work, giving him a few choices. He chose a desk on his own next to hers and in a corner so he was, in effect, enclosed on three sides. He wanted to stay there when the rest of the children were on the mat and she agreed, saying that, when he felt ready, he could join them. This actually gave him the opportunity to maintain his self-image as being an outsider *without having first to do something wrong.* It also gave him the power to erode this self-image by joining the rest of the group when he felt ready.
- Since he had missed so many pre-reading skills she arranged for two parents to come in and read stories to B for 20 minutes twice a week. She also organised a rota of Year 6 pupils who volunteered to read stories to him for 10 or 15 minutes every lunch time. This had the additional benefits of shortening the length of unstructured time at lunch when he could get into trouble and helping him to get to know some older pupils who could be friendly and helpful in the playground.
- She developed a number of activities he could work on fairly independently and at which he could succeed. For example, for maths she prepared sheets with pictures of different numbers of small items, say, one pen, two rubbers, three pencils, or one red cube, two blue, three green. The task was to place the correct number of items on the picture. Using different coloured cubes, numbers were gradually introduced in this way and led on to simple addition.
- Any piece of work done or attempted well and any behaviour reasonable for him were praised warmly and he was awarded stickers liberally. When he had received 10 he went to show the head teacher who awarded him a special star.
- The teacher gave him small tasks to carry out with other members of the class who were most likely to be cooperative and helpful, for example, taking the register to the office, tidying up the pencil tray. The aim of this was to help B succeed in being helpful and to get to know some class members in a positive context.
- The teacher started to build up a relationship with B's mother, seeing her regularly and talking to her about his successes so that she, too, could gradually gain new expectations about his behaviour and ability to learn. B was very proud to show her his sticker book. The teacher also pointed out the sorts of books B would be bringing home daily and asked his mother if she could spend ten minutes at home reading the stories or talking about the pictures with him.

In this way the teacher gradually and consistently helped B to see himself in a new light and to accept that new self-image. By half term, she had started to give him the opportunity of working with one or two members of the class in various activities and a different parent now read to him and two others. By Easter, he joined the rest of the class on the mat on most occasions, but still could retreat to his desk if he felt the need. Some days were definitely better than others but, on the whole, he made steady improvement. At transition to Year 1, the Reception teacher briefed his new one about his needs and her strategies and these were continued. By Christmas he was receiving help from the school's learning support team and, although he had difficulties, he was making progress. Socially he had made great strides, despite occasional fights in the playground. He had made two particular friends and was able to work in class quite cooperatively with a few others. At the end of his first year, he played a minor, non-speaking role in the Christmas performance well and got enthusiastic applause: he had successfully integrated into the class and seemed a much happier boy in school.

Let us consider what exactly a teacher needs in general terms in order to manage a pupil who, like B, exhibits unacceptable behaviour and to help him or her accept a new self-image.

1. An understanding of the behaviour; what exactly is it saying or showing? This involves an understanding of the child's script and of the role offered to the teacher. It is not necessary to know about the pupil's home life or past experiences since his or her behaviour and body posture speak for themselves and provide the key to understanding enough with which to work.
2. An understanding of your own feelings. How do you feel about the child? Is this how you usually feel about children? Is this a kind of behaviour which triggers particular feelings in you? Or could it perhaps be how the pupil might feel? For example, most teachers, even those who were usually very patient, felt extremely angry and frustrated about a certain boy in Year 7. In time it was discovered that he had difficulty hearing. It seemed that, feeling angry and frustrated at not being able to communicate easily, he behaved in ways which invited similar feelings in others.
3. An ability to stand back and not take things personally; this can be difficult since the child's behaviour can at times feel like a very personal attack. This perception can be strengthened if the pupil behaves more acceptably with other teachers, but not with you.
4. A sense that it is the child's behaviour that is unacceptable, rather than the child themselves, and that behaviour can be changed.
5. An awareness of at least one area in which the pupil can already gain praise, for example, attendance, punctuality, one subject area in which he or she manages with less conflict, etc.
6. To present work and behaviour tasks which can be achieved.
7. To give consistent reinforcement that the child is fine, though the behaviour may need changing in very specific ways.
8. Persistence and patience.

In the example concerning B, the first three points above enabled the teacher to think independently, that is to say, to perceive the child's behaviour outside the script. If she had felt personally targeted or had thought that the pupil was aiming to make her life difficult, then she would not have been able to offer him a new self-image and would have remained part of the script.

The teacher was able, however, to stand outside the script and consider the behaviour and what it was saying about B's world view and self-image. This enabled her to maintain an approach throughout the intervention which was consistently free from blame, even though it made clear that the unwanted behaviour was unacceptable. The emphasis was always on what B could do successfully and on redirecting his actions rather than on his unwanted behaviour. This might be described but not interpreted since interpretations are likely to fit in with the script. So, for example, the teacher might say if B looked about to hit a classmate, 'No, B, we don't hit. Be gentle. Come and show me your lovely work.' She would avoid saying something along the lines of, 'Stop frightening Emma, B', or 'Don't be a bully', or 'Don't be naughty'.

Sometimes it can be quite threatening for a pupil's world view to be challenged and his or her behaviour may at first become more extreme for a while or he or she may use avoidance tactics of some kind. In this case, the fact that the teacher allowed B to remain in his desk when the others were on the mat seemed extremely helpful since he could retreat into his former self-image of being separate and different if he needed: he was in charge of the pace of change.

The following is an account given to me by a highly effective teacher describing how she dealt with a boy in her class who had quite severe behavioural and learning difficulties.

> My memory of X before he came into my class was that he was often quite high profile, sitting outside the classroom at break because he had not managed to do what was expected of him. I think he never felt that anyone was very pleased with him or smiled at him properly or praised him. That is how he presented himself to me. He had a classroom assistant who was actually quite brusque in the way that she dealt with him and the things that she said. A record book went to the parents every day and it was a catalogue of horrible things, 'X has bitten this child, X has kicked me, X has punched me, X has sworn at me', and so on, and I knew this would be very upsetting to receive as a parent.
>
> If X was wandering off or interfering with someone's work the teacher and classroom assistant had sometimes held him by his clothes. I did not think this was very nice. If you want to hold onto a child because they are misbehaving you can actually hold their hand. They see this as acceptable because it is the kind of thing people do when they are being kind to you. Holding onto somebody's clothes is quite different. By holding their hand you get the response you want and they can interpret it in a much better way. I think grabbing someone's clothes is antagonistic and guaranteed to cause problems.
>
> X was not allowed to have books because, it was said, he ripped them up and wrote in them. He had to work from photocopies. I would have liked to change that. It was yet another way in which he was made to feel different for negative

reasons rather than positive ones: he did not even have a proper book.

When I got him in Year 3 I think it was my sense of survival, my intuition and my experience as a mother that helped in dealing with him. I really had to make this work for my own personal survival and it never occurred to me to try to do so in an aggressive way.

I knew making the boundaries too close for someone like X was going to be a disaster for all of us because there was no chance of his succeeding. The boundaries needed to be in place, and very firmly in place, but much wider than for other children.

I thought the communication with X's family was really important. If they felt he was doing well then they would be nice to him and praise him and then he would come in feeling more positive. I could see that the whole thing could be turned around, but I did not know how it could because I had no experience at the time. It was just a feeling that something had to be better than what was actually going on. As a parent myself, I found the way his parents had been treated offended me enormously. If that were my child and every single night the report book said he had not done anything nice I would not want to come into the school at all. The teachers said his parents never stopped to talk and did not seem interested. It was not a lack of interest, they were just acutely embarrassed. Once I started to say things like, 'We've had a really good day and he's done some nice work' they were prepared to come and chat and say how they felt about things. They had their own fears and worries. It was difficult for the family to cope with having a child who was not 'normal'. It was harder still then to find that the school seemed to be against him. I felt so sorry for all of them. He had been set up for failure all the time.

So I kept a daily book but I started writing nice things about him even if he had done horrible things. At the beginning he did kick me, with his boots on, and he did do all sorts of horrendous things to me. But every night I wrote, 'X did a lovely piece of work today', or something similar, and when his parents came in I would show them a piece of work and make a big thing about anything good that he had done.

It just seemed to change in some way in front of me: suddenly there was this nice little boy who did not need to sit outside the staffroom. He was never going to be the same as everybody else. He was different. There was no way that he could conform in the same way that others did. It was useless to even expect him to. Gradually he stopped being high profile in assemblies. He would do nice things like he would come and sit by my feet just to be with me. He obviously felt quite secure, quite sure nothing was going to go wrong if we stayed together. In the mornings for registration he would sit on the floor on a cushion leaning on my legs and that is where he felt quite happy. It was quite important for him that when we were on the carpet that he could come and sit in that position. I also made a special place for him in the class by moving a table so he was in a corner enclosed on three sides. When his classroom assistant sat in the entrance he was totally enclosed. This seemed to give him a sense of security while preventing him from wandering around the room. He and the classroom assistant had special cushions and I decorated the walls around him nicely.

The other thing with X was that I had a very clear routine for him which he got to know quite quickly. It did require quite a lot of extra work. He knew he sat on the carpet with me for register first of all. While the other children were doing their early work activities two children then took it in turns to play an educational game with him. Once he understood what was to happen he would always get himself organised for this. I think he quite enjoyed the security of his own personal routine. Personal routines for disruptive pupils are important so that they have their own structure which might be totally different from other children's in the class. They need their routine and their routine needs to be maintained since they lack the maturity to cope with change. That is when supply teachers can have difficulty.

Things changed quite quickly. Certainly by the Christmas. The family all seemed to be happy that he was obviously much more settled. Everything improved. I cannot believe that having a battle with anybody like X is ever worth the energy. It just is not. The children's responses to X improved and his inter-actions with them were much better. Certainly in the last two terms there was no kicking and spitting and punching. It was really so simple to do when I talk about it like this. He had special treatment. He was very different, a unique child, of course he had to have special treatment. I suppose some people could have said that this was favouritism because he got away with things other children did not get away with. But the curious thing is that the other children accepted it. They knew that he was special. They knew why he got away with certain things and they did not. So it never caused a problem. Nobody ever said, 'How come you let X do that but you don't let us do it?' Not once in a million years did anyone ever question what was going on.

I did all this intuitively. I suppose I always go for the easy option. I cannot see the point in having battles, especially with some poor little seven-year-old with special needs. Why? To prove what? Being afraid that you cannot control children can be a dangerous thing in teaching. You are in control because your relationships are good and that is where the control comes in. But that also means that the children have a say too: it is not a one-sided operation. Relationships are always two-sided. You are not going to let the children walk over you or stop you asserting sanctions if necessary but this is better coming from a base of good relationships rather than bad ones.

X left to attend a special school after the year with me. I saw him a couple of years later when he came to a school fair. He did not come over and talk to me, though he said, 'Hullo'. At one point, he looked at me and just gave me this little sideways smile. And I thought, 'You do know me. I did have an impact. I did make an impression. You haven't forgotten. It is all there. I did make a difference.'

The outcome in this case was extremely positive. It might be useful to consider some of the steps the teacher took. She:

- Considered what school might feel like for X and his parents and reflected on what approach would work most effectively.
- Formed a relationship with the parents and helped change their perception of X.
- Took charge of the relationship with X and ensured that it would be a positive one, despite his early behaviour.

- Set boundaries and tasks for X which he could manage and through this helped him change his own self-image. In other words, she set up the kind of boundaries and tasks that meant he could succeed rather than setting them up so he failed.
- Accepted X unconditionally even though some of his behaviour was unacceptable. This helped X realise that he could please others and could be liked.
- Gave X the safety of his own routine and his own special space at his desk and when sitting on the carpet. She kept him close to her so that he would feel safer.
- Acknowledged his differences by helping him feel special rather than defective.
- Allowed him to take charge of his learning when possible, for example, by organising the morning game himself.
- Helped X form relationships with other class members by arranging for them to spend time together in very structured ways.
- Persevered and was patient.

The power of thinking

Children's perceptions of themselves have been discussed in Chapter 2 in relation to learning basic literacy skills. Here I would like to consider from a different perspective the role of thinking about ourselves in relation to how we act.

There is a way of standing or sitting and thinking in martial arts in which a person is 'centred', in other words, balanced and relaxed with his or her energy flowing. When in this position it is very difficult to be pushed over, not because you are resisting any pressure but because your energy is radiating out. It is in this state that a martial artist can break a brick with his or her bare hands. When in this state, a person is relaxed, alert, confident, powerful and unshakable both physically and mentally. That is to say, *being centred is the best preparation for having to do any physical or mental work*.

In the martial art aikido, for example, there are several ways of reaching this cented state:

1. 'Keeping one point'. This refers to the practice of keeping the attention on the movement centre, hara or dan tien, which is to be found in the centre of the body three or four finger widths below the navel.
2. Relaxing completely.
3. Imagining your energy radiating our from your hara.

Another way of 'keeping one point' is to think of yourself doing something well, using whichever primary representational system is strongest for you: for example, in your mind's eye *seeing* yourself doing something well, getting the *feeling* you have when you do a particular thing well or *hearing* a phrase associated with doing something well. In other words, *thinking you can do something well, in whichever way is most natural to you, is a way of equipping yourself to perform as well as possible*. If, for example, your primary representational system is visual, then getting a picture of doing something well will be most empowering; if it is kinaesthetic, then experiencing the feeling of doing well will have most effect, and so on. With a little thought, this may seem obvious. However, there are two additional points which it may be useful to consider.

1. Thinking about doing something badly has the opposite effect, namely, it uncentres you. In this state a person can more easily be pushed or pulled off balance

both physically and emotionally. A common example of this is sports men and women losing their nerve after a small mistake and going on to perform worse and worse. An image, a feeling, or a sound or phrase associated with failure uncentres them and they loose the poise, balance and focus which makes success possible.

2. If children hold a deep belief that they are stupid, naughty, noisy, bad at maths, art, games or writing stories, etc., then it will be difficult for them, whatever their strongest representational system might be, to imagine themselves doing those particular things well. It will be difficult for them to imagine themselves understanding and thinking clearly, being good, being quiet, doing maths, art, games or writing stories well and with ease. Since they perceive themselves in negative terms they will remain emotionally and physically uncentred at some level and are unlikely to achieve as well as they could. This line of thinking leads us to three further points.

- The central importance of building pupils' self-esteem, confidence and emotional well-being in the classroom.
- The value of using constructive rather than labelling criticism. This is discussed in the section below.
- Sometimes it can be useful to help pupils change their body posture, in other words, help them to stand, sit or move differently in order to facilitate a change in how they behave or work. This might be as a part of their adopting a role which will make it easier for them to work or behave differently or might simply be by paying attention to their stance. One boy with SpLD in Year 8 hated humanities and spent the lesson hunched over the desk. This posture reinforced his sense of being 'uncentred' and unable to manage in the lesson. In science, however, which he loved, he sat straight and alert. Consciously employing the latter stance for humanities enabled him to manage a little better and certainly to feel slightly more confident.

Building confidence and self-esteem while 'telling off': using constructive criticism

It is often quite difficult at times to persist in using constructive criticism, *describing* a pupil's behaviour rather than *interpreting* it. If a child has caused you trouble and disrupted your plans it is understandable that you might want to blame him or her. Though tempting, this might, in the long run, cause you even more trouble since it may well reinforce a pupil's negative self-image and make a change in behaviour more difficult. If a child is labelled, for example, as 'naughty' or 'bad' this can be problematic in at least three ways:

- such labels tend to be very unspecific, meaning very different things to different people;
- labels stick – children may well come to identify with the label, they think they really are, 'naughty', or 'bad'; it is much more difficult to change the kind of person you are than a specific behaviour; changing from being 'bad' to 'good' is, therefore, a much harder task than to change behaviour in specific ways, sitting still, listening carefully, helping your neighbour;

- other people, other teachers, classroom assistants and the rest of the class can begin to accept the label too, expecting the child to be 'naughty' or 'bad'; this also makes it harder for the child to change his or her behaviour.

Consequently, it can be more helpful to all concerned to persevere in focusing on what the pupil can do and to continue redirecting him or her towards desirable behaviour. This is an approach in which boundaries are maintained firmly and kindly, and hope remains alive for the pupil. Meetings with parents or carers are handled sensitively so that the child is not humiliated, particularly in front of peers.

What is true for individuals is true for whole classes. A class that is regularly told that it is noisy is likely to believe this to be the case and become more so. One that is frequently called helpful or cooperative may well improve. Obviously, it is not appropriate to lie, praising children for being quiet or working well together if this is patently not true. If the class have gained a bad reputation then it is worth mentioning this, adding that, with you in charge, you feel sure they will be able to show everyone how well they can work and behave: you are there to help and guide them. It is also possible to emphasise positive behaviour while pointing out areas needing improvement. For example, the first approach below is more likely to produce a cooperative response than the second.

- 'Well done for tidying away so quickly. That was brilliant. Now, this week I'd like you all to notice any noise you make when tidying up and to be as quiet as possible. I'll remind you next time so that you'll be not only quick but quiet too. That would be even better than today. Now sit down as quietly as you can and we'll see just how well you can do.'
- 'That was awful! You were all making so much noise. Now sit down in silence.'

As individual examples, the difference in these approaches may not seem that great. However, when you consider the accumulative effect of either approach, all day, all week, all year, you can appreciate that the experience of being on the receiving end would be very different indeed. The first tends to value effort and small improvements while encouraging specific changes in behaviour. It appears to be based on a confidence that the pupils will succeed and are cooperative. It empowers the children. It points out in small stages what needs to be done next in order to improve. It offers hope. The second tells off and blames, leaving no room for the pupils to show they can do better. Over time it tends to disempower.

3. Reversing the downwards spiral: helping children change

Even in primary school you may have some pupils who are quite cynical about authority and anti-school. Others will have very deep beliefs about themselves which are unhelpful and which have very entrenched behaviour patterns associated with them. Helping children change their behaviour is often, therefore, a quite difficult and lengthy process.

Anyone who has ever tried to change his or her behaviour, an old habit of some kind, will probably appreciate just how difficult it can be. Yet we often tend to expect children to turn over a new leaf, to try harder or to be good without appreciating or spelling out the detail of just *how* that is possible. At the time, the child may sincerely wish to change, but when a similar situation next arises he or she slips back into the old, undesirable behaviour. Desire alone, however sincere, is often insufficient: more is needed if change is to be lasting. Indeed, there are at least five ingredients vital for change: a genuine desire to change, detailed knowledge of *how* to do so, that is, what to do instead, a change in self-image, practice and perseverence.

The ideas which follow can be adapted as necessary to suit individual children and different ages. It is often helpful if a teacher from another class becomes a child's main support or mentor. The class teacher ensures boundaries are maintained while the colleague takes an additional interest in the child and gives encouragement.

L had been the 'naughty boy' in his class since he had arrived in Year 5. Unfortunately the school had lacked a positive behaviour policy and the teacher had dealt with him as best she could, often sending him out of class to work in the head teacher's room. Now, at the beginning of Year 6, L's behaviour was more difficult to contain: at the end of year trip the previous summer he had been the only child in the school who was forbidden to attend the outing because of poor behaviour. L had maintained that he 'didn't care!'. Now the school had a positive behaviour policy in place and the Year 6 teacher was determined to put time and effort into attempting to help L change his behaviour before secondary school. L's home life had been very difficult and he lived with his grandmother who was sympathetic towards the school but was at her wits end regarding L's behaviour.

In class, L was very demanding of attention, shouting out answers, questions or comments rather than putting up his hand during whole-class sessions. He found it difficult to remain on task for more than a few minutes at a time, after which he would display a range of disruptive behaviour: getting up to chat to someone over the other side of the class, wandering about, punching another pupil, tripping someone up. He had no particular friend and at playtimes often became involved in fights. His work was far behind many in his year, and he received help out of class with the school's special needs teacher for three quarters of an hour each week. One-to-one he generally worked well since there were no peers to distract him, he had help immediately whenever he needed it, the teacher could bring him back on task when his attention wandered and he received the constant attention and frequent praise he seemed to crave.

The teacher thought carefully about some of L's behaviour which seemed difficult to control and decided the best thing to do was to try not to control it but to put it in a different context, one in which it was permissible. He had a sense that L himself might feel uncontrollable or out of control and, therefore, needed a structure which would help him to feel he was in charge of his own behaviour. In time, this might help change his deep beliefs about himself.

Consequently, the teacher drew up a plan targeting L's most disruptive behaviour first, namely getting up and disturbing other pupils when working individually or in groups. This included a meeting with L, his grandmother and the special needs teacher in which they agreed a contract with L. In this meeting the teacher asked L where he thought he could best work, sitting alone, or with a particular person. L wished to work alone, as close to the teacher's desk as possible. The teacher suggested that L had a five-minute egg-timer on his desk so that at the end of each five minutes he could get up and go to show him his work. In this way he was incorporating L's need to move into a behaviour which was sanctioned. This also gave him regular, brief attention without misbehaving. The teacher would praise his efforts and direct him to the next piece of work. Although this required considerable teacher input it was no more than L demanded anyway, the difference being that this was a positive interaction and L was learning he could win attention by following the rules set up. If he managed to get to the teacher and back without disturbing anyone the teacher would stamp his special card.

L could go to see the special needs teacher every day for the first five minutes of lunch time to show her how he had got on and to let her see his work. Since he worked well with her individually, her approval was beginning to matter as the relationship developed. If he had not managed to get many stamps she could encourage him for the afternoon and praise any work done or effort he had made. She had observed him in class and had noticed that he became easily distracted by gazing about. His thoughts seemed to follow his vision and when moving around the classroom he tended to wander off in whatever direction he looked. She suggested he imagined a small, safe place for himself to work in when in class, perhaps a cave or a snug part of a room at home. He said when he was little he would hide under the table at home. She asked him to imagine he was under the table and all he had with him was his work and the egg-timer. When the sand had sifted through he could peep out, spot the teacher and, keeping his eyes on him, take his work to show him.

On Fridays, L was to go to the head teacher and show her some of his best work that week. This was to enable the head to develop a different relationship with L since he was now seeing her for a positive reason, not to be told off. L's grandmother came in once a week to see L's work and his special card with stamps.

When this programme was started the class teacher told the rest of the class and asked them to help L change his behaviour and to support him in his efforts. This they generally did. The teacher gave L a 'buddy', a quiet boy who worked well and was able to make friends easily. The teacher paired them up whenever possible, in PE, for art activities, for doing jobs. She gave them responsibility for keeping the class pencils sharpened and tidied.

Breaktimes, especially lunch times could still be problematic since L found unstructured time most difficult to manage without getting into fights or annoying others. His teacher suggested he helped a classroom assistant who employed some juniors to look after children in Reception. L did this well. He had a specific role and could help the smaller children. He also received attention himself from the assistant. Twice a week L and B read stories to some of the children in Reception.

The contract drawn up between L, his grandmother, his class teacher and the special needs teacher had four targets for L. These were:

- to arrive in class on time in the morning (which he always did);
- to look after the pencils with B (which he managed easily and enjoyed);

- to show his teacher his work every five minutes and return to his seat (the target behaviour);
- to do one really good piece of work (another major aim, to help L feel more confident about work and more interested in it).

In return for this, he would get attention from his class teacher when L showed him his work, from the special needs teacher at lunch time and from his grandmother when she visited the school each week. L's target was always set at a level lower than his teacher thought he could manage so that success was inevitable. At first, he needed to get ten stamps a week. This was gradually increased. Also, he began to do more than one piece of good work a week. L's 'reward' was to be a weekly certificate from the head teacher acknowledging his improved behaviour and work. His grandmother proudly stuck these on the wall at home. His class was to go on a theatre trip at the end of term and, if he had at least six certificates he was to be allowed to go. He could also gain ten minutes a day special time when he could choose what to do from a guided choice of three possibilities.

L's behaviour did not improve overnight but, gradually, he began to believe he could behave differently. He gradually acquired a different kind of experience in school: he did not have to be the 'naughty boy' of the class to gain attention or a special role. He could improve his behaviour and be helpful. He went on the theatre trip and at the end of term all the juniors who had helped Reception children at lunch times were applauded in assembly and given cards made by the children. This gave L some very public praise.

Progress continued steadily. During the spring term L was to show his work to his teacher every ten minutes. He sometimes forgot to do so. The teacher suggested he now put his hand up for attention, rather than getting out of his seat to find him. After Easter, L asked to stop using the egg-timer and put his hand up when he wanted help. He now had a watch which he had been given for his birthday and sometimes timed himself. In the second half of the summer term, however, L began to get into fights again and to disturb the class in ways he had not for some time. His teacher thought this was L's fear about leaving for secondary school and talked to him about it. Although the teacher was preparing the class for the transition he thought L needed a little more support and arranged a special meeting for him with the head of special needs at his new school and his future form tutor. During this meeting, L's teacher outlined his difficulties and his huge progress over the year. This alerted the new school to L's vulnerability as well as his ability to change. It provided the opportunity for L to start a relationship with his new form tutor in a positive way.

The sensitive and comprehensive nature of this teacher's programme for helping L change is a reminder that telling children to 'behave', or 'be good' or increasing the severity of punishments for misdemeanours is frequently insufficient if we really want to help them change their behaviour. As the professionals, it is up to us to find a way of helping pupils improve their behaviour if they cannot do it alone, and they often cannot. L's teacher attempted to provide:

- Sufficient support and encouragement with the help of the special needs teacher, L's grandmother and the head teacher so that L did not feel the task of changing was too difficult or that he was on his own.
- Specific targets which he could usually achieve and which gradually became more demanding. In this way success was more likely than failure. The fact that the contract was written down made the targets more tangible. L could see that, although he had to do something, so did everyone else involved.
- The opportunity to build on the relationship with the special needs teacher and gain her approval; also the chance of changing the nature of L's relationship with the head teacher.
- Rewards which became more meaningful to L as time went on, such as praise and approval, the opportunity of joining the class outing, choice.
- Understanding about the process of change. It was accepted that change does not occur overnight and that L might have setbacks, especially when there was an alteration to the routine.
- Opportunities to change his beliefs about himself and to develop a more positive self-image. *It is the way we think about ourselves and the world that shapes behaviour. A lasting change in behaviour will always include a change in thinking, a new self-image.*
- Some consistency. This was possible since three staff members were involved in supporting L so that if one was absent another could probably step in to help. The teacher also made links with individuals in his new school to ease the transition to secondary. Some level of consistency and emotional safety is important because without it change is unlikely. In many cases, change can be challenging and frightening and the risk involved may seem daunting. When frightened, people tend to hang on to the familiar; it is not a time to try out new behaviour. Consequently, the safer the emotional environment around a child in school and, indeed, at home, the more possible change will be.
- A new habit, alternative behaviour which was within the school rules and helped L work and grow in confidence.
- Attention for positive reasons, rather than for poor behaviour.

Rather than focusing on stopping poor behaviour, the emphasis is perhaps more effectively placed on concentrating on developing the desired behaviour, that is to say, on instilling a new habit. For example, rather than thinking about not talking in assembly, a pupil would be given specific things to listen out for or to notice during that time and a new body posture to practise.

However hard you, the teacher try, however skilful you are and however carefully you think things through, interventions are unlikely to be successful all the time. Some issues are out of our hands and, ultimately, you can merely do your best, referring on to relevant agencies where necessary and facilitating change where possible.

Offering skills and practice: introducing the idea of choice

Many children repeat behaviour even though it is unwanted and gets them into trouble *simply because they do not know what else to do*. Telling a child to 'be good' or 'behave properly' is often far too vague to be helpful since being good and behaving properly can mean many different things to different people! Even more specific intructions such as 'be quiet' or 'sit still and listen' will be insufficient for many children since they need to know *how* to be quiet or *how* to sit still and listen; they need to know *what to do instead* of the behaviour that is unwanted. Telling them to be quiet misses out some important steps along the way. Just think how difficult it is as an adult to behave differently: you have the good intentions, but when a similar situation arises you invariably fall into the old patterns of behaviour. Habits are difficult to break. Stopping a certain kind of behaviour is extremely difficult without recognition of the following:

- why you are doing something;
- what you get out of the behaviour;
- at what point you start that pattern of behaviour, the 'trigger';
- a technique for creating a gap between the 'trigger' and the behaviour to be changed, a gap in which you can choose a different path, a moment of choice;
- an alternative behaviour, something to do instead;
- support, encouragement and praise;
- a strategy for helping you persevere when you fail to create the gap and slip back into the old behaviour.

Skills for creating a moment of choice are, in particular, frequently omitted.

The following 'what if?' exercise can help introduce the idea of choice about actions. It reinforces the distinction that behaviour is separate from who we are, that *behaviour can be chosen.* Consequently, change is possible, it simply requires a different choice and the skill and perseverence to carry that choice through.

The teacher starts off by suggesting a possible scenario. For example, *'What if Sarah jostles Tom when lining up for lunch. What could Tom do?'* For some scenarios, pupils could volunteer to take roles, without actually hitting each other, of course. The class suggests what Tom could do. The consequences of each line of action are traced and discussed, including how participants might end up feeling. For example, Tom hits Sarah back: what might happen next? Tom tells a teacher, ignores the jostle, and so on.

Potential scenarios could come from pupils themselves. Alternatively, an episode from a story could be used as the starting point. The exercise can be adapted to suit the age of the children.

Follow-up exercises can entail an exploration of *how* you take up a new behaviour. *How* do you remain calm rather than immediately assuming that someone who jostles you in a queue is meaning to hurt you, so you do not instantly hit them back and get into trouble? *How* do you get on with your work instead of chatting to a neighbour when he or she starts talking to you?

What might be suggested, discussed and practised here are the specific requirements for the process of change.

- The pupils identify the trigger for the response, and what they might feel, see or hear prior to that response, in other words, their internal signal that the possibly unwanted behaviour will follow. They have already explored alternative responses.

- Next come the skills for creating enough space to choose a different behaviour from the habitual one: breathing, shifting position and relaxing. It is at this point that determination and will can be particularly helpful: the child chooses the desirable behaviour. Each time he or she does so, the next decision will be a little easier.
- Then comes the alternative behaviour which has been chosen.
- Reflection on how they might feel about the consequences of this behaviour as opposed to those following their former behaviour.

All this can be practised: instead of instantly hitting back, a child might breathe, step back, relax, choose and then ask why the other pupil jostled him or her. The class watching can prompt and help. The child who has been playing the role of the one chatting can, once she or he notices the old pattern, breathe and shift into a position which is attentive for work. In this body posture chatting will be less likely. Once issues have been discussed and explored in such a way, there is a quick reference point whenever the unwanted behaviour occurs. These exercises can be easily adapted for use in small groups or with individuals.

Helping a whole class to change: turning a class around

It may be necessary to reverse a downward spiral of poor behaviour, demoralisation and disaffection of not just an individual but of a whole class. At some time you may be faced with taking on a class with the reputation of being the most disruptive and the hardest to teach in the school. The children will probably be fully aware of their reputation in such cases. Taking over a class who, for whatever reason, have had a number of teachers in a year or over the past few years can also present a problem. Part of the difficulty here may well be that some children are more wary of building up a relationship with a teacher if there is a pattern of instability. The children most likely to disrupt are usually those least able to manage change and they often fare least well with a series of new teachers. A very experienced and highly effective teacher and deputy head, Sheila Stone, gave the following suggestions for turning a class around from one which is considered disruptive and uncooperative to one which cooperates well and works effectively together.

> To change the behaviour of insecure or ill at ease children, as opposed to simply containing them, you need to change their self-perception. Constraint and punishment will not do this; it will only reinforce negative, resentful feelings. What an adult needs to do is to make the child feel good.
>
> If they [the class] . . . believe in themselves they will not only not want to let you down, but they will not want to let themselves down either. They will have gained self-respect.
>
> Studies have shown that the most effective way of dealing with bullies is for the children to join together and decide to exclude someone who behaves in this way. It is more effective than individual discussion or behavioural programmes. You and a core of children can set the code of behaviour that will be good for the class as a whole and challenge anyone who 'spoils' it for the rest of the class.

1. Establish a code of behaviour

The school will have its own code of behaviour. Take five or six of these points crucial for the smooth-running of the class and use them as the basis of a discussion about behaviour they would want and expect. When you decide on your 'rules' make them positive. They need to be something the children can do, not things they are not allowed to do. (For example, 'Listen to others' rather than 'No interrupting'.) Whenever possible, use the children's own words. As they have played a part in devising the expectations they are more likely to respect them themselves and help each other maintain them. This erodes the notion of discipline being the teacher versus the pupils. It is more a question of the teacher or another pupil pointing out that anyone not meeting the expectations is spoiling something for everybody. *In this way, teacher and children are on the same side.* This is particularly important in a class which has been misbehaving, since it is usually the case that when the children are not squabbling or telling on each other, they will be ganging up in some way against the teacher. Creating expectations which are for the benefit of and to be safeguarded by all helps create different relationships between the children and between them and the teacher.

Here are our school rules:
Children and adults should:

- Speak politely to others and listen to them.
- Be kind, considerate and helpful.
- Work hard and try their best.
- Use equipment sensibly and take care of the environment.
- Be aware of other people's space and need for privacy.

Display these rules prominently for all to see.

Two things children most hate in teachers' behaviour are shouting and making a loud noise, such as slamming a register down on a table. (The thing they most like is helping them with their work.) Children need to feel that their teacher is strong. This does not mean giving conditions and punishments. It means taking command, taking responsibility, sorting things out so that they are safe. One of the ways you do this is by establishing a structure or framework within which they can operate safely and confidently. This involves the following points 2 to 7.

2. Establish routines

This is important so that the children know where they are and what they have to do. They are, therefore, more secure and settled. A pattern of procedures and routines frees the teacher since he or she does not have to make a new decision each time a situation arises, the routine takes over. Another advantage is that the system can carry on even if the class teacher is absent, thereby minimising disruption to the class. Examples of routines are:

- Early morning work, so the children come in and straight away get on with something, leaving no space to run around, argue, tease, etc.
- Activities for the children to do when they have finished a piece of work.

- Folding clothes and putting them on the desk after you change for PE.
- Knowing where to put homework.
- Knowing what to do if you are absent and so miss information given.
- Knowing how letters are given out.
- Ten minutes silent reading after lunch.
- Ten minutes handwriting after play.

3. Let the children know what will happen during the day
You can organise this differently depending on the age of the children. It is useful to have a weekly timetable displayed in the classroom. A copy can be sent home to parents and carers the week before, listing at the bottom the equipment required for each day. This has many advantages. It enables the children to take responsibility for organising themselves and frame their day. They can be more independent, knowing where and when things will happen. They will learn to manage time as they become used to meeting deadlines. As with routines, knowing what will happen next helps children feel more secure. Run through the day's timetable each morning or through half a day with younger children.

4. Explain
It is often assumed that children know why they should or should not do something. This is not always the case and it is worth explaining why the expectations are in place; for example, why it is better to stand still when lining up rather than pushing others.

5. Keep tight structures: have seating and lining up arrangements
Have planned seating arrangements for tables and also for sitting on the mat. This minimises disagreements and also ensures children are sitting in places which will most help them concentrate. Children who seek attention must need it, so put them at the front where they will get lots of it. At the front you can smile at them and can whisper if they are getting out of hand. Children with any hearing loss or poor eyesight need to be where they can hear and see well and have eye contact with the teacher. If left to choose their own place on the mat, those with special needs of any kind will often want to be at the back. Usually they attend best when in the middle of the group where they can see the teacher or the board directly in front of them. In the middle, they will not feel on the fringe of learning.

A list for the order in which children line up to leave class, assembly or the playground can be useful. This again minimises potential disagreements. It also makes it easy to check if someone is missing, such as those who sneak to the toilets on the way back to class. It provides the children with another opportunity for taking responsibility for organising themselves: they know the order and it is up to them to get into line correctly without the teacher telling them. You could put an attention-seeking child in charge, right at the front. Then tell them they are a good leader. This gives this child a sense of responsibility and a reason to behave since being first in line has status. It suggests that he or she is to be trusted, which makes it more likely that he or she will be trustworthy. If this appears not to be the case, the teacher can then say something along the lines of, 'If you can't be trusted, you'll have to go further down the line,' as a warning, not a threat.

6. Classroom organisation

The layout of the classroom is very important and has to suit your own personal needs. It must also be such that:

- when the class are working and you wish to get their attention everyone can see you easily;
- all can comfortably see the board and any other displays necessary for a task;
- those who are less able are closer to the board or whatever they are working from so that they can look up and down quickly without distraction. They could even have their own copy to work from;
- the tables are not too close so that children can get up without knocking into each other;
- everyone has enough room to work without bumping into a neighbour;
- all children can look forward towards the board if they are working from it. This will probably require at least part of the classroom to be in rows with as many tables of two as possible. From an early age children can work silently from the board. Tables can be rearranged for group work.

All equipment needs to be logically organised, clean and labelled. Unsettled classes usually have children who get up and wander around instead of working. Children should get everything they need for an activity at the beginning of the lesson so they do not engage in mindless wandering or cross-group socialising. Ensure someone sharpens the pencils each day so there are always spares. Teach the class how to correct their work without using rubbers.

Always:

- have some regular activities available which some children can get on with independently, for example, a spelling box, so that you are free to work with others;
- orchestrate praise, sometimes by devising 'tricks'. You could say you have to pop out and wonder if the class can sit quietly for a minute. Arrange beforehand for a colleague to walk past as if by chance and praise the children. Send for the head teacher to look at good work or to praise children for their behaviour;
- ensure the children are quiet before they come into the room;
- have the children tidy up and leave the room in an orderly fashion. Leave enough time for this.

Never:

- send children to sit at a table without some activity to do;
- keep children waiting to do their work while you are explaining a task to another group;
- send the whole class from the carpet to activities. Send them a group at a time.

7. Establish what kind of lesson it is to be

Is it one where they listen to the teacher who will explain or one where they exchange ideas to gain understanding? Tell them what the learning objective is. For example, 'In this lesson we are going to learn that matter does not vanish, it merely changes into something else. In order to understand this we . . .'.

Let the children know what to expect and what is expected of them. Establish when they can talk and at what level. Some activities are to be done by themselves, quietly, for others they will need to talk; sometimes the teacher will talk and they will need to listen and put their hands up to ask questions, and so on. Ensure the children know what type of response is expected of them.

8. When and how to group children

Most children work happily and well when they are sitting with people they like and feel comfortable with. If the work in class is differentiated, they may need to be in groups so that they can share resources, discuss ideas, work cooperatively on the same task, or be taught by the teacher as a group. This ability grouping can be efficient. Often children are put in groups when they do not need to be. Or they are put into groups in one subject because they are good at another. For example, the top science group may consist of good readers who can record well, rather than those who can think scientifically. Care should be taken in selecting appropriate ways of recording results or testing understanding. A child wrongly grouped could easily loose motivation.

9. Assess, observe and be well informed

In order to manage a class you have to know and understand individual children. Therefore, it is useful to find out as much as possible about the children before starting to teach a class. Read records, speak to the previous teacher, the deputy head and SENCO to become as well informed as possible. Observe the children and get to know them as soon as you can. Use spelling and reading tests to set work that matches pupils' ability and interests. Much unacceptable behaviour results from the fact that work is at an inappropriate level so fails to engage the individual.

10. Ensure turns are taken fairly

Since a class that is in disarray will almost certainly have poor relationships between pupils it is important to avoid potential disputes by ensuring that all turns are taken fairly. Have lists for turns displayed and ticked off so everyone can see it is fair. Start the list sometimes at the beginning of the register, sometimes at the end and work backwards and sometimes in the middle, working forwards or backwards.

11. Consider how you present yourself and what you say

Smile. Use your voice sensibly. Raise it to gain attention and then drop it immediately. The louder or higher your voice gets the more the children pick up your tension. You can use a show of anger to tell children off for something serious but do not loose your temper otherwise you will no longer appear to be in command of the situation. Remember you are in role.

Use humour when you can. You do not always have to be right in every situation. Sometimes the children will be. So acknowledge this and apologise if appropriate. Praise given must be praise meant. Do not say something is good if it is not. If you say 'good' to everything, the children will not believe it. Explain why you are praising something, 'Good work, you listened carefully and have included the main points in your work' or 'That was quick. You must have been practising at home'.

12. Punishments and rewards

As mentioned earlier, the aim is to help children feel good about themselves again by remodelling their self-image. Positively reinforcing good behaviour is the most effective way of doing this.

Some teachers write up the names of good pupils on the board. Some put a smiley face on one side under which they note those who have behaved and/or worked well and a sad face under which they note those who have not. In a sense, this sets up an expectation that some children will misbehave or fail to work well. We should want everyone of them to feel we expect good of them. A clean slate is very freeing. You could say, 'You're now my class. I like you and I'm not going to have you mess about. I don't care if others say you're naughty because I know you can show them you're not. My classes always help one another and work well and I know you will too.'

Rewards: Children often like something to recognise that they have tried hard and achieved. Stickers on work are popular, so are stickers on clothes. Once this becomes competitive, as in a star chart, an element of devisiveness is introduced into the class. Star charts tend to undervalue most children in the class who get on and work well, over-emphasising the achievements of those of high ability and those who have behaved poorly and are trying to improve. This demotivates the majority who resent the others and relationships within the class deteriorate. So if you use stickers, use them wisely, and sparingly – and always personally so they measure themselves against themselves, not against others.

Punishments: These often do not match the crime, build up resentment and estrange the individual concerned. Whole class punishments rarely work and you are seen to be unfair and controlling. It is far more effective if someone has misbehaved to say, 'What is the matter?' (pause for a reply) 'This is not like you. I expect good behaviour and you have let yourself down.' Or, if a reason is given, 'Now I understand, but you were wrong. Next time, how do you think you should handle this?'

I usually give children a choice: to decide to behave in the way expected of them or, if not, to expect me to do something to stop the unwanted behaviour. If, for example, they are talking to a friend, I would separate them if they did not stop talking or move of their own accord. If, on the mat someone was jostling a neighbour, I would get him or her to sit elsewhere if he or she did not stop after I had pointed out the choice. The children seem to accept this approach as fair.

13. Relieve tension

Find a colleague with whom you can discuss your frustrations and triumphs and who will respond sensitively. Much poor behaviour results from children feeling tense because they cannot do the work and/or because they or other members of the class have not been behaving well. Strategies that help relieve tension can, therefore, be of use. Anything that is fun can work, like a dressing up day, for example.

14. Unwanted behaviour

Once the class as a whole has settled down as a result of your organisation and earlier strategies, you can focus on the unwanted behaviour of individuals. Fine tune your assessment and analyse what they need. Monitor their behaviour. Avoid even thinking about them as 'bad' boys or girls.

Children need to be involved in managing their own behaviour. They usually recognise their difficulties and want to improve. Having the confidence to admit that they need help is a brave thing to do. It is helpful for teachers to recognise this and let the child know. Once there is this understanding and trust, children will want teachers to help. They need boundaries and objectives. One way is to write a plan. You should decide on targets with them. A target could be, 'I will start to work straight away and not get distracted.' The teacher and child monitor this on a chart.

If a child has difficulty behaving when the class teacher is not present (for example, at playtime), another member of staff such as one of the support staff could be the child's mentor and friend. It is important the child chooses who he or she wants for this role.

15. Maintaining motivation

Being a good teacher is more than delivering a fine lesson with objectives clearly met. It involves transporting the children beyond the ordinary. Enthusiasm is catching. It is enticing, interesting and involving. It can inspire the children. If the work is interesting and exciting, the class will have no need to misbehave.

Success is the greatest of all motivators. Interesting work that is matched to the children's needs and abilities is absorbing and satisfying. Recognition is another wonderful motivator. Stickers and certificates, praise and privileges do this. But I've found choice to be the biggest 'carrot' of all. Choice allows the development of independence and personal freedom. If you have high expectations, when these have been met allow the child to choose an activity he or she enjoys. Giving extra work as a 'reward' to those who complete work quickly and well can be a great disincentive to getting finished early. Good choices could be: time on the computer, craft activities, drawing, playing a game such as Monopoly, jobs.

A complete surprise can lift the spirits of the whole class and leave them feeling good about themselves. This might, for example, be suddenly deciding to go and play a game with them because they had all been sitting quietly or had worked so well.

A personal study talk to the class is an effective way of helping children feel more enthusiastic about school. The children take turns, one a day, to give a talk about their passion at the time. Topics range hugely and can include such specific items as narrow guage railways and mackerel fishing. The children talk about their subject and then manage a brief question time, taking no more than ten minutes in all. This exercise provides children with the opportunity to learn about one another and to listen and ask questions in a responsible fashion. The teacher can learn a great deal about the individuals in the class by observing this process.

16. A positive class ethos
The children need help to gain a corporate feeling, a sense of joint responsibility and a liking for each other. Once they all feel they are achieving individually but not at the expense of anyone else they will get on better together and be able to be more generous spirited with one another. Anything that helps individuals and the class feel good about themselves will encourage that sense of cooperation. Regular class meetings with established codes of behaviour are a good forum for discussing important aspects of human relationships and getting on well together. A whole-school curriculum planned for this is ideal. Subjects discussed could include, jealousy, difference, possessions. It can be helpful to have a box of books in the classroom specifically about feelings and emotional issues. Children can read these and use them as a starting point for discussion.

It is helpful not to pretend that everyone is the same and to speak openly about differences. Something hidden can be a worry. Once in the open it can be recognised and supported. So one could say something like, 'So-and-so has difficulty with spelling. But never mind, we're all going to help him this year,' or, 'So-and-so has a temper, but it's okay. I'm in charge. No one will tease her about it and we'll all help this year.' Children can then relax if they are embarrassed about their difference and do not need to try to cover up and pretend. They also know they will be helped and supported. The others learn to be a little more understanding and accepting.

17. Modelling learning and behaviour
Model learning and behaviour in all you do. Talk through the process as you are doing something. So if it is mental arithmetic, ask how different children arrive at their answer. Explain how you do and compare the differences. If the children have to read silently, sit and read silently yourself. Treat the children with respect and listen to them, so they will do this to you and each other. Shouting at children to be quiet is, of course, the classic contradiction.

18. Regular information to parents and carers
Meet parents and carers as soon as possible so that you can build up rapport and so that the children know that you are working together. Write to parents explaining how they can help with homework. Have a regular homework book. Have tasks which can mostly be corrected at home and involve the parents whenever possible. For example, in the instructions ask parents to tick the work, show the children how to do something, write certain words, and so on.

19. Step by step

Do not try everything at once. If there are going to be changes, tell the children and limit the number of changes at any one time. Be flexible, patient and persevere.

The following incident illustrates how Sheila Stone, the teacher who provides the above suggestions, interacts with children, successfully using choice rather than punishment as a means of improving behaviour. In doing this, she helps build children's self-esteem rather than diminishing it.

Two girls sat talking throughout assembly. At the end, the teacher quietly spoke to them. She then pointed out that they had been talking and said that they had a decision to make before the next assembly. They had to decide whether to sit separately or, if they wanted to sit together, to sit quietly. If they sat together and talked, she would have to move them. She asked them what they wanted to choose. They looked at each other and decided to sit together without talking. The teacher said they had made a good decision.

At the next assembly they did not talk. The teacher noted this and gave a smile of approval. They were also aware that, if they talked in future, the teacher would move them. She had allowed them to make their own decision, however, so it was in their interests to sit without talking.

Using this approach the teacher:

- spoke quietly and respectfully to the children so they were not humiliated in front of the class;
- outlined the three options available to them and the consequences if they sat together and talked, leaving them to make the choice for themselves;
- treated them with respect throughout, giving them the responsibility of making the decision about their own behaviour.

If they did talk in future and were moved they could not blame the teacher for being unfair since they had let themselves down by failing to carry through their decision successfully: in this case the temptation of talking to a friend would have been stronger than their resolution. By dealing with the matter in this way, the teacher avoided conflict and possible future resentment while giving the girls the opportunity of improving their behaviour through choice. She empowered them through choice rather than simply telling them off without the chance of putting things right.

Preventing troublesome behaviour

A major theme of this book is how to avoid troublesome behaviour by maintaining pupils' motivation, making success inevitable, emphasising an ethos of mutual respect and building confidence and self-esteem. Whole-school approaches for avoiding troublesome behaviour include constructive strategies for playtimes, some of which are outlined earlier. Some schools develop a positive behaviour policy which supports, teaches and models the kinds of communication and social skills which promote collaborative learning and more peaceful relationships between pupils. The ethos of these schools is one of tolerance and cooperation and the pupils are offered the skills and guidance to meet such expectations. For example, one secondary school is promoting the idea of pupils being charming and pleasant, the staff modelling this amongst themselves and in their dealings with pupils. Lessons are sometimes videoed. The pupils subsequently watch them, discussing their behaviour and how they could help each other work more effectively.

This chapter has dealt with:

Juggling

Troublesome behaviour

- What is a teacher's role?
- Getting an understanding
- Disruptive or reasonable?
- A different approach: offering a new self-image
- The power of thinking
- Building confidence and self-esteem while 'telling off': using constructive criticism

Reversing the downwards spiral: helping children change

- Offering skills and practice: introducing the idea of choice
- Helping a whole class to change: turning a class around
- Preventing troublesome behaviour.

Chapter 6

Finding your way

One thing is certain – what we believe will determine what and how we teach.

(E. B. Castle, *Ancient Education and Today*, 1961)

This world is not the same to all people. Each one lives in his own little domain
. . . Peace and harmony may reign in one person's world; strife and war in
another's. But whatever be the circumstances of one's environment, it consists of
both an inner world and an outer world. The outside world is the one in which
your life engages in action and interaction. The world inside of you determines
your happiness or unhappiness.

(Paramahansa Yogananda, *Inner Peace*, 1999)

1. Developing your own style

Inner authority

Confidence in teaching is often linked to a belief in our own authority as a teacher,
that we do, indeed, have the right to take charge of the process in the classroom and
make things happen. Developing and maintaining a sense of inner authority can be
a gradual process and is promoted by certain ways of thinking about ourselves. This
thinking includes at least three elements.

- A belief that children can be trusted, that they will listen and carry out the
  instructions you give, that is to say, they will accept that you are in charge.
- A belief that you have the right as a teacher to make demands and be in charge of
  the process in the classroom and that this is necessary in order to maintain
  respect for all and to foster learning, understanding and independence.
- No *need* to be liked by the pupils. Obviously, if you are liked it is pleasing, but
  you are not *dependent* on pupil approval or this can cloud your judgement. You
  are likely to be popular if you enjoy teaching and being around children, if pupils
  feel respected by you and each other in your class, if there is a sense of order and
  demands and expectations are clear, if the children can develop independence, if
  it is possible to succeed and if the content and/or process of the lesson is
  interesting.

It often requires a considerable degree of confidence in order to feel sure about your own style of teaching. This is particularly true when beginning teaching, moving to a new school which may have a different ethos and approach from one you have worked in previously, taking over a class from a popular teacher with a contrasting personal style or when working alongside such a colleague. It is often tempting to try to adopt strategies and approaches that colleagues use successfully. Indeed, it is extremely helpful to keep an open mind and to take on board good practice observed or discussed. As a teacher you never stop learning about how to teach more effectively: it really is a question of lifelong learning. There needs, however, to be a word of warning here since there is a crucial, though sometimes subtle difference between trying to be like someone else and using a colleague as a role model, in other words, adopting techniques, strategies and approaches and making them your own. Let us consider these in a little more detail.

Trying to be someone else

An example from a secondary school will illustrate my point. Early on in my teaching career I had to share a Year 9 tutor group with another teacher whose style was very different from my own. I had to take the register on two days, she did so on the remaining three. She had been the sole tutor for two years and had clearly established how things were to be done: the register was to be taken in total silence, the pupils sitting still, waiting for their name to be called. With greater experience and/or confidence in my own authority it would have been possible to establish my way of doing things despite the obvious testing of boundaries which usually occurs when a new teacher takes over. I would have liked to have a book box so that pupils read silently for ten minutes while I went round, making contact with the new class, learning names and taking the register as I went. Unfortunately, I lacked the confidence to do this and thought I ought to be the same as my colleague. This was a dismal failure since I lacked the inner conviction to carry through her style. When I used the same words she used, instead of falling silent the class took little notice. They sensed, quite rightly, that my heart was not in it. And it certainly was not: it was like wearing someone else's clothes without making the style my own, I felt and clearly appeared uncomfortable.

Taking on a role model with conviction
With more knowledge, I could have learnt much from this teacher by using her as a role model. To do this I would have needed to do several things with very conscious intention. For example:

- decide what seemed most effective in her style of classroom management;
- analyse the differences in our approaches; note what she did differently and how it was different; consider the kind of relationship this would be likely to develop with pupils;
- consider the differences regarding expectations and rules and decide which of these I could embrace;
- pinpoint what I would find most difficult to carry through with conviction and choose whether to take these aspects on board anyway or alter them to suit my style;

- notice in some detail her body posture and practise sitting, standing and moving as she did, that is to say, practise entering into the target body posture wholeheartedly, entering into role; note how differently I felt as a result;
- notice her voice, how she used it and where it seemed to resonate from in her body; practise speaking using her kind of body posture and use of voice; consider if I could carry this off with conviction;
- feel convinced that this was the most effective approach with a particular class.

If I had done all this I could have extended my range of skills so that with some classes, or with some young people in some situations, I could have drawn on a different approach as necessary. This would have been effective, however, only if I had felt convinced that this was the best approach and had quite systematically considered the different aspects involved, as outlined above. I would also need to have changed aspects with which I felt uncomfortable so that I could carry the whole approach through with conviction. The change in body posture is usually important here. Without all this, the result was, in fact, very ineffectual.

Constructive noise is okay
It can be particularly difficult to develop the confidence to allow a certain amount of noise in the classroom at times, especially if there are colleagues who maintain quiet. Obviously silence is sometimes crucial, especially for some activites, when someone is talking to the whole class, for example, when children are working on a task which requires individual concentration and during silent reading. At these times it can be less distracting to others if a child asks the teacher a question rather than a peer.

However, pair or group work requires discussion about the task. As we have seen in Chapter 2, the stage of thinking and talking about a subject when children can explore ideas together and clarify their own is often a vital preparation for writing. Yet it is sometimes omitted, perhaps because it inevitably leads to noise. Although children may conscientiously start off whispering or talking quietly in pair or group work, their voices usually raise as they get more interested in the topic and more involved in the what they are doing. Animated discussion on task usually indicates work is going ahead well.

It is perhaps worth remembering that if an activity is interesting, relevant, at the appropriate level and sufficiently well structured and clear then pupils usually stay very much on task and their talk is relevant to the issue in hand. They stray away from the task and start chatting, taunting each other and even fighting when the activity is boring, irrelevant to them, too difficult or too easy, poorly explained or when preparation has been insufficient, very often the exploratory discussion and thinking stage having been left out. If you find pupils have been wandering off task then it is generally worth considering how it can be made more appropriate or accessible before assuming they are being wilfully disobedient.

It is a useful classroom management technique to help children understand that sometimes it is appropriate to be silent while at other times constructive talking is fruitful. Confidence in your ability to allow noise sometimes and to curtail it swiftly and effectively when necessary often reflects a solid sense of inner authority.

In turn, this sense makes it easier to achieve silence immediately when children are noisy and excited. This can be especially difficult at certain times, following or preceding a treat, for example, leading up to Christmas, after an unusual event, a trip, sports day, during windy weather or on wet days when there is no outdoor play, and so on.

Building confidence: developing a positive physical presence

One of the challenges or part of the excitement of teaching, depending on how you view it, is the immediacy of it all: your time never seems your own. The bell rings and you know the children are lining up expecting you there or are coming into the classroom whether you are ready or not. It can be very intense, the pace at times seeming relentless. The children are looking to you to shape the day and if there is to be a quiet, calm time then it is up to you to make it happen. This is particularly difficult to do when you are feeling rushed, flustered or anxious yourself. Any ways you can find to stay calm, stay in touch, stay 'centred' can, therefore, be extremely useful, especially for those moments when your carefully-laid plans are foiled by the Unexpected.

The Unexpected, in the guise of a change in schedule, a video machine not working, an assistant who is crucial for your plans being absent, and so on is common in schools. The more flexible and relaxed a teacher can be in unexpected circumstances the more he or she can help calm down the most vulnerable pupils who find any kind of change difficult. It can also be very helpful to the children to model a calm response to the Unexpected which is based on flexibility and an ability to problem-solve at short notice.

Two ways of developing a relaxed, calming presence in the classroom are

1. to adopt a role;
2. to pay attention to your breathing and physical stance.

1. Adopting a role may entail using a teacher as a role model as outlined above, or may involve using the same technique to model yourself on anyone else, even a fictional character, who possesses suitable qualities and presence.

2. This technique for developing physical confidence can help create a sense of inner authority. This can be particularly helpful if, for whatever reason, you are feeling vulnerable, insecure, unconfident, or simply ill or tired.

To use this approach train yourself to check your posture and your breathing whenever you can, for example, before, during and after you or the children enter the classroom, when dealing with a difficulty, at times you think things are about to get out of hand, after a challenging incident. How do you stand, sit and move in order to feel most at ease in the classroom? How can you use your stance to help you feel quietly confident?

In checking your posture, notice three key areas:

- your contact with the ground;
- your face and neck;
- your chest, which includes your breathing and your voice.

When anxious, many people tend to have poor contact with the ground, hovering from foot to foot, or will have their weight very unevenly balanced. Others may have their toes curled as they grip the floor tightly. Both these stances can give the impression to others that you are ill at ease and that you do not feel comfortably in charge of the situation. Children may well sense this, even if they are not consciously aware of it. Particularly those who are most emotionally vulnerable need a teacher who appears comfortable and confident.

It can be helpful to check and readjust your posture as necessary whenever you remember:

- Shift your posture so that you feel yourself standing or sitting in a relaxed way supported by the floor or chair and yet upright and alert, with the sense of having your head in the clouds and your feet firmly on the ground.
- Relax your shoulders by feeling the elbows are heavy and soften any tension in the chest.
- With the mouth closed, do some pretend yawns. This relaxes the throat and diaphragm.
- Remember to keep breathing. Take a breath deep within you and, as you breathe out, feel or imagine a wave of relaxation sweeping over you from head to toe and out through the soles of your feet, taking with it all tension. Take two more breaths in a similar way. Then breathe as you do when you are relaxed and alert.
- Think of an image, a word or two, a sound or a feeling which instantly helps you to feel calm, relaxed and able to manage with ease.
- An alternative way of getting into a confident stance is to practise 'centring' as described in Chapter 5.

Breathing patterns change with our moods, any tension reflecting in a different kind of breathing as we hold our breath, or breathe more shallowly, more deeply, quicker or slower. Bringing our breathing back to a pattern we use when feeling relaxed, centred and alert and bringing our stance to our most comfortable appropriate posture is a quick way of recovering our equanimity at difficult moments.

From such a physical stance it is easier to respond in a relaxed way. It is also easier to think and choose, before rushing in with a habitual response which may not be helpful. From this relaxed, alert and calm position you can reach out with your voice and eyes to any point in the room in order to gather attention to you. You come across as relaxed, safe and in charge without appearing either aggressive or weak.

As with any training, best results are obtained by relaxed practice at times outside the situation itself. A growing awareness of how body posture and breathing can influence your communication and feelings can thus be usefully developed and reinforced at your leisure.

Using your voice

The voice can be a powerful tool for teachers. It can convey warmth, approval, disapproval, enthusiasm, fear, anger, etc. At times of stress and high anxiety in particular, it might let us down, revealing all too clearly the insecurity of the moment. What we intend being a calm instruction might turn out to be far more feeble, squeaky or wrathful than we would wish. We can feel exposed and undermined, let down by our voice. Yet we can use it, too, in a way that can help build our confidence and sense of personal power.

The first point is about structure. If the chest and throat are relaxed and we are breathing with some comfort, our voices can flow more easily. Trouble often arises when there is considerable tension across the chest, shoulders and throat. This can inhibit voice production. To have a relaxed chest and powerful voice the legs, feet and diaphragm must be relaxed, and we must be breathing easily.

The second point concerns where we focus. Often when aware of having to project our voice we concentrate on our throat itself and on the 'target', the person or people we are addressing. This can limit our voice considerably, especially if our throat is tense. If, instead, we imagine our voice starting from the lower abdomen, the 'hara' or 'dan tien' described in the previous chapter, and flowing out through us, beyond those we are addressing to infinity, the effect can be startlingly different. Rather than limiting ourselves, we are facilitating the energy within the voice to flow out from us. Another image might be that of a dart sent from a blow pipe. We are the pipe and we shoot out the energy dart with ease. It is less a question of volume here and more one of intensity.

Fostering intuition

One way of helping to develop a secure sense of your own inner authority is to foster and trust your own intuition, in other words, your ability to know or perceive something or to get an insight without using reason, intelligence or information gained through the senses: you just know. Using intuition in teaching can add an inner confidence in your decision-making abilities. It can help you choose between what you think you ought to do and what you know will work. In Chapter 3, the teacher was instinctively acting upon her intuition when she let one girl call out. In the section 'Juggling' in Chapter 5, the teacher who allowed Y to draw and build with blocks and Lego was using her experience and perception, guided by her intuitive understanding of him. An effective actor or actress responds intuitively to the audience, going beyond the mechanical delivery of a speech in order to touch, inspire and take everyone along with him or her. When a teacher uses intuition in this way he or she is going beyond the sterile delivery of the curriculum and is truly practising the art of teaching.

In thinking about intuition, there are several points to consider:

- everyone has intuition, some people use it more than others;
- intuition can be developed, the more you acknowledge it in small matters, the easier it is to trust at more difficult or important times;
- one obstacle to trusting intuition can be a diffidence in distinguishing it from habits in thinking or behaving and from fears; it can be useful to ask yourself, 'Is this really my intuition or is it a habitual way of thinking or behaving, or a familiar fear? Do I often think this kind of thing?';
- working as a professional, it is important to question intuitive ideas against reason, perception and experience; intuition cannot be used as an 'excuse' for

doing whatever 'feels right'; it is a calm sense of knowing something rather than feeling something.

Time spent in contact with your own inner source of replenishment and regeneration, your quiet place, can help the easy recognition and acknowledgement of intuition. This can be found in different ways by different people, meditating, cycling, etc.

Refining skills

Continuous learning

As teachers, we expect children to seek knowledge and understanding, to learn, reflect, continually improve their skills and develop into increasingly mature human beings. We are more likely to inspire our pupils to do this if we model the approach ourselves, that is, if we continue to refine our skills, reflect on our practice and give time and attention to personal development. However much you know in teaching, there is always more to learn. Since teaching involves forming relationships with all the children in the class and finding ways to individualise learning and unlock each child's potential the task of devising new solutions to new problems is never-ending. This is not as daunting as it sounds: *each child in your class can always help you learn something new.*

If a child is not interested in school work or is not progressing as expected then there are two immediate lines of enquiry:

- Do we need to be doing something differently: relating differently, providing other work maybe, or putting work across in a new way? Or maybe all three? Have we understood how this child best learns and what might inspire him or her? What else could we do, and how?
- Does he or she have a particular difficulty with work or with relationships in the class? Is there a temporary or ongoing problem outside school affecting him or her? Is this a period of consolidation and emotional development during which academic progress slows down? Is there a learning difficulty of some kind?

In both cases, would it be useful to talk to him or her, to a parent or carer, or to the teacher from an earlier year. What else could we do other than monitor the situation?

We need constantly to be questioning and refining our process of teaching, using the children's development and attitude as our feedback. Inspectors aside, how would the *children* rate our performance? What would *they* get out of being in our class? Thinking along these lines, we can maintain our own level of motivation and success as teachers.

Increasing efficiency

Teaching can be divided into two major areas: firstly, administration, planning and marking and, secondly, the process of teaching and relating to pupils. Earlier chapters are devoted to the second point. Here I would like to focus on increasing efficiency in the first area since this can help develop confidence and a general sense of coping. If feeling overwhelmed by the administrative workload it is easy to resort to an authoritarian approach in an attempt to control the children themselves rather than staying on top of administrative tasks and feeling in charge of the process of teaching. This can lead to a deterioration in relationships with pupils, a drop in children's motivation and a decrease in teacher confidence. Spending some time refining administrative skills can, therefore, be very worthwhile.

Discrimination and prioritisation

Although making a list of all that needs to be done can be helpful since it relieves us of the burden of having to remember everything, it can also be extremely depressing. This is particularly true if the list is long. It is also often difficult to know where to start, the temptation being to flit from one task to another without finishing any. The busier we are the more likely this is and the cycle is thus worsened. A more helpful approach can be to categorise the list from the start by placing tasks under the following, or similar headings:

To be done this week; next week; this half term; next half term; next term; this year; if it were a perfect world.

Some tasks might get shunted down the list as the time limit elapses. Some may even find themselves in the last category. This is an invaluable one since it very often highlights our creative desires, maybe also our unrealistic expectations or high level of demands on ourselves. If there is no time for tasks in this column then it is easy to feel deeply frustrated since what we really want to do as a creative contribution in our work is left undone. If we have high personal demands then rarely tackling this column can erode confidence. Conversely, if we concentrate on the final column without completing essentials to be done in the near future, again it is easy to lose confidence since we may not manage even everyday demands.

You will not do any less work if you categorise tasks and the chances are you will do more. The significant difference is perhaps that you will worry less about what is not done and have more energy for the task in hand.

Once you have tasks planned in this way, at any one point you have only *this week's* agenda on which to focus. The work needed for the current week can then be planned on a daily basis, setting *realistic* goals for each day and spreading the load through the week. Adding a few items you have nearly completed and which can be crossed off early on can help make a promising start.

Prioritise. Who needs this work doing: you, the children, your immediate boss, the school, the government? What are the consequences if you do not do it today? You then can choose your priorities. Once choosing you are taking responsibility for the consequences and accepting your own area of power within external constraints.

Apportioning time

One way of improving efficiency with a heavy administrative workload is to break up tasks into manageable chunks. As we tell children to structure stories and essays with a beginning, a middle and an end, so we can divide up both tasks and time. Rather than avoiding a mountain of work too big to attempt you can separate out tasks into more manageable chunks and allot portions of time to them.

Once you have a plan of action, work through it systematically. *Concentrate on one thing at a time.* If you have not finished a task in the time allotted make another decision. How much longer might it take to complete? Would it be best to do that now or later? Choose as you go along. Experiment with the idea of time outside of work. Try different approaches and see what is most effective for you. What is your best time for working? What helps you feel confident in the way you use time? What system serves you best? The concept of managing time by apportioning it for specific activities can often help to develop a sense of being in charge and a conviction that, if you keep at something long enough, often enough, in small enough chunks, even the most enormous of tasks, even report writing, can be completed. The better we can manage time ourselves the more we can help our pupils to do so too.

We can also consciously use positive, clear intentions to improve our efficiency. Before starting a piece of work, for example, we could think something along the lines of, 'I want to do this well in the shortest time possible', or 'I want to finish this in fifteen minutes.' This is likely to help our concentration much more than vague thoughts such as, 'I suppose I'd better get this done . . .'.

Intention can be used in any situation. If meeting a parent, it could be helpful to set out with a definite intention of really listening and making contact with him or her. If attending a training session, the intention could be to understand and retain the most important points made. If starting to teach a new class, it could be to perceive each individual in the class and to start a fruitful working relationship with him or her. To use intention effectively, concentrate very deeply for a few moments before beginning the task in question, on the way to a meeting or to the classroom for example, and then forget about it and become absorbed in the particular activity.

Our thinking is powerful, more powerful than we often give it credit for. It also strengthens with practice. If at first you notice little difference, then try it again until you do. It may take a little time to establish positive intentions in the place of unclear, masked and maybe unhelpful ones, but the more you use it the greater its effect will become.

Developing confidence: a change in thinking

Developing confidence in a new area of work often requires a change in thinking about ourselves, an alternative internal self-image. Choosing a positive role model can again be of use in acquiring new ways of thinking about ourselves.

We developed a self-image when we were very young. This will now seem very familiar to us and may have been altered and updated as a result of various experiences and our response to them. It may not, however, always be one which will support us most as a teacher. What do you consider the most fundamental qualities of a good enough teacher? Which of these do you already possess and how can you develop the rest? Who does possess them and how can you use this model as a way of growing into the role of an effective, experienced and confident teacher?

2. Maintaining motivation

Finding satisfaction

It can sometimes be hard when teaching to feel satisfied, to feel as though you have really achieved something and left a job well done. There are several reasons for this. Let us consider two of them for a moment and what can be done, despite them, to derive a sense of satisfaction at work done well enough.

1. One reason is the fact that the workload is so huge, there always seems to be something else that should or could be done. And this is just to cope with the everyday demands of trying to motivate and individualise learning for some 30 pupils, never mind all the ways in which resources could be developed and education could be improved! A job which never seems completed or done to your own personal satisfaction can, over time, have a very demoralising effect. Just as pupils need to finish a piece of work and gain satisfaction from their achievement in order to maintain their motivation, so do teachers. Since this does not naturally occur in teaching it is important to create it in some way for yourself in order to remain enthusiastic, energised and motivated. The following are some ideas for doing so.

- Focus on what you have done, rather than on what you have not yet done. Often we get this the other way round, quickly passing over our achievements and focusing on the growing mountain of tasks awaiting us. Whatever we direct our attention towards tends to grow in our mind's eye. Thinking about doing a task many times before beginning it results, in a sense, in our doing it several times over.
- Keep a notebook handy and jot down all you need to do as you think of it. In this way you free yourself from having to keep it in your head. Consult your notebook when prioritising and planning.
- Keep things in perspective by using careful prioritisation as discussed more fully above.
- Make a *realistic* daily list of all that needs to be done.

2. Another element of the work which makes it difficult to perceive your input and derive satisfaction from it is the nature of children's development. Children do not progress in a steady, linear fashion. They may have periods of quiet consolidation and then sudden bursts of perceptible progress. Thus on a day-to-day and week-to-week basis it is often impossible to assess a pupil's development in relation to your own input. There are too many variables: your hard work and ability to motivate may bear fruit a few months later on; conversely, if a child was very unhappy with a previous teacher's style this might set him or her back for some time in the future, and so on. This is true even without taking into consideration a child's personal preferences and interests and all the ups and downs of friendships, home life and simply growing up which also affect the speed and nature of development. However, stepping back a little and looking at six months and the whole year at a time, it is sometimes more possible to gain some idea of how children in your class have developed. Ways of doing so, which can also be helpful to pupils, include:

- Taking a sample of work completed in a set time and comparing it with a similar timed task halfway through and/or at the end of the year. Discuss the difference with the children individually. Observe the process, in other words, how pupils go about their work: are they more or less confident, organised, purposeful, enthusiastic, more or less likely to offer an answer or take part in a group activity?

- Observing relationships: are the children more or less cooperative working in a group, are they able to resolve conflict, make or retain friends? Do they engage with teachers and visiting adults?
- Asking what the children think, how they feel and what they have observed about their progress. At the beginning of the year, they can be asked about their anxieties for the year and what they are looking forward to, what they enjoy and dislike, what they want to learn, skills they would like to develop, and so on, depending on their age. At the end, they can comment on what they have learnt, skills they have developed, what has changed for them at school, how confident they feel, etc. This can be done in various ways, for example by asking pupils to write it down, by taping or videoing a class discussion or pupils interviewing each other. Videoing is particularly effective since pupils can really get a sense of how they are growing up. As a teacher, too, you may notice things which indicate that a child has developed in very important ways, for example he or she stands straighter, is able to speak more confidentally, has made a real friend. Such indicators of progress may not, of course, show up on test scores.

Avoiding disaffection: managing stress

When adverseley affected by stress it is very easy to feel disaffected with work as a teacher partly as a result of tiredness and and partly because there seems too much to do. Developing techniques for managing stress can help with this, as can building support systems which enable you to flourish, as well as the children in your class.

There are many external demands which have been discussed earlier. Usually there are also certain internal demands. These are our own expectations of how we think we should carry out our work and relate to others. What do you expect from yourself? How hard are you on yourself when you think you have made a mistake? Does your thinking support you or add to the hurdles to be jumped?

Internal demands are beliefs about the way we think we *ought* to behave, which may be conscious or unconscious. We may, for example, be aware that we are a perfectionist, that we feel anxious if we are even a few minutes late, that we find it difficult not to win, or that we get upset if others are arguing. We may not, however, be aware that we have other demands driving us from the unconscious. These are not obvious, but when looking at the pattern of a life they may become clearer. The fact that we may never be satisfied with ourselves whatever we do, for example, may point to a belief that we have to be perfect or have to succeed.

Internal demands of this nature can be about anything. For example: 'I must be good, perfect, brave, beautiful, entertaining, busy, calm or cheerful', etc. 'I must hurry up', 'I must try harder', 'I must do my best', 'I must keep troubles to myself', 'I must stand on my own two feet', 'I must succeed', 'I must get it right', 'I must please others', 'I must make it all right for everyone'.

Such demands add an extra pressure on top of any external demands we are facing in our work. They keep us trying harder and harder, driven by the fear of not matching up to our own standards. They can erode confidence and contribute to our levels of stress. What is true for teachers is, of course, equally true for pupils who will also often be driven by conscious and unconscious internal demands.

Stress is a natural part of life since it is inherent in our response to any stimulus, our response to change. Consequently, *it is not necessarily damaging.* Research illustrates two points:

- There are very similar physiological processes present in the body whether something happens we consider good or there is an event we consider bad. What is interesting, however, is that the former will be much less damaging to us than the latter. *It is how we perceive life events, as good or bad, our perception of things, which seems to determine the degree of damage we experience.* Our thinking is, therefore, very powerful.
- The more stressful jobs are those in which demands are great and in which an individual has little control. However, since the harmful effects of stress depend largely on our perception of events, that is, our attitude to what happens, some people suffer more from stress in a similar kind of work than some of their colleagues. The significant factors which seem to influence the degree of susceptibility or resilience to suffering from stress are:

Control – how much control people have in work or how much they *perceive* themselves having. Those who have more control or who feel they have control are less adversely affected by stress.

Confidence – viewing change or potential difficulties optimistically. People with this approach tend to have confidence in their own resources to meet new experiences. Change is not immediately regarded as a threat, burden or problem, but rather as an opportunity to be met.

Commitment – people feel supported and find something meaningful in their work or life.

Thus we find that the crucial elements seem to be:

- a confidence in one's own resources, that is, a sense of inner authority;
- finding meaning in what you do, finding satisfaction;
- the ability to be aware of the control and choices one does have in a given situation;
- feeling supported.

The first two points have been discussed earlier this chapter. Consideration of the last two follow shortly.

Considering habit
If we tend, first and foremost, to perceive a change as a demand on our time and energy or a new task as a problem, a burden or threat, this may be partly due to habit. If you have such a habit, here is one way you can start developing a more relaxed approach.

1. Start to notice as early as possible when you are feeling stressed.
2. Ask yourself if this is, in part, due to an old pattern of immediately perceiving a change, a new situation or a demand as a threat, a burden or a problem.
3. Take a deep breath in, relax as you breathe out and feel your feet on the ground. Take a few steps back mentally from the situation. Review it from a different perspective. See how it sounds and feels from there. Is it really, *in the present,* such a burden, threat or problem?
4. How would it be if it were an opportunity instead? What might you lose? What might you gain? Who do you know who might consider it an opportunity? How would he or she sit or stand? Get into that position and see what it feels like. If you do not know anyone who fits this description, or, if it feels more comfortable, get into the posture you imagine someone would have with that frame of mind. (Remember that all new behaviour inevitably feels a little strange.)
5. In this new posture ask yourself what personal qualities you could employ or develop in taking this opportunity. Tell yourself that you could try out a new approach. Imagine how differently you could see things, talk about the situation or feel about it.
6. You may not want to change anything. Simply experiment with the possibilities: 'What if I were to . . .'.

Exercising choice
It often seems that, to do a teaching job as well as you could, it would require there to be at least 25 hours in a day and eight days in a week. Consequently a major skill for avoiding disaffection and minimising distress from stress is to discriminate and prioritise as mentioned earlier this chapter, and to feel confident with your choice. Since being aware of having a choice in any situation is an antidote to feeling powerless and suffering from stress, another useful skill is to find areas for personal choice and opportunities for exercising initiative and control within frameworks which, at first glance perhaps, seem to offer little room for individualisation. It can be helpful, therefore, to enjoy the opportunities for choice that are available, rather than focusing on what cannot be changed. When something is inevitable or has to be done then the only choice remaining is that of our attitude, in other words, how we relate to it: can we embrace it wholeheartedly, or do we continue to resent it? Remembering that choosing is empowering, can in itself sometimes minimise stress.

Learning to unwind
If you are stressed then it is helpful to recognise this as quickly as possible and have techniques for unwinding. The more familiar we are as teachers with noticing our emotional state and learning to change it into one which is more supportive to ourselves and what we are endeavouring to achieve in the classroom, the more we can help those children who become entrenched in some kind of unhelpful behaviour to do the same. The first difficulty in dealing with stress is noticing that you are suffering from it since it is often easy to be so involved in the detail of the day that you become stressed without realising it. The earlier you notice your familiar symptoms the better: becoming aware of habits without judgement is the

first part of change. With practice it is possible to spot how you in particular react when stressed:

- How do you feel physically and emotionally when becoming stressed?
- Are there any key phrases you catch yourself saying that might alert you? For example, 'I've got so much to do . . .', 'I haven't time for that now . . .', Just leave me alone . . .'.
- What kind of thinking accompanies, or immediately precedes your feeling stressed?
- Are there any situations or times in the week or term which you tend to find particularly stressful?
- Check your posture for tension, take a deep breathe in, relax as you breathe out and shift your position as described earlier this chapter in the section on developing a positive physical presence.

The more frequently you check for stress and then relax, the more time you will spend in a calmer state. Gradually that state, rather than being a stressed one, will become the norm. Patience and perseverence are useful in this. If you forget to check and have been stressed for some time before you notice, relax anyway. It is impossible to experience emotional and mental stress at the same time as deep physical relaxation. Being relaxed and yet alert can help both concentration and efficiency.

Support systems and balance: care for the carers

Teaching is a demanding job and it is easy to become over-stretched and burn out. To avoid this it can be fruitful to consider how you are going to:

- maintain your own sense of enthusiasm, enjoyment and inspiration in working with children;
- build a support system for yourself, a network of people who can provide personal and professional support on a regular basis: a support system ensures that you can discuss concerns, air ideas and talk about incidents to help you unwind;
- find emotional and intellectual nourishment and creative satisfaction;
- maintain a balanced lifestyle; creating a balance of rest, exercise, food and interests not connected with work;
- develop strategies to unwind and recover from stress.

Cultivating calm

If we expect the children in our class to sit quietly and peacefully then we can often best help them to do so by developing our own capacity for calm. The more confident and calm we not only appear but actually feel, the more we can lead by example and the more likely we are to create a sense of peace around us. Whatever it takes for you to cultivate internal calm can greatly help your effectiveness as a teacher. Developing a sense of physical presence described earlier in this chapter can promote this by building a solid stance. So also can making time each day for a little quiet.

3. Summing up

What the children say

A group of boys and girls in Year 4 were asked to list the qualities they considered most important in a teacher. They agreed amongst themselves that a 'good' teacher:

- makes the work interesting;
- treats you with respect, is nice to you;
- listens to your point of view;
- listens to everyone when sorting out an incident;
- doesn't shout;
- lets you go to the toilet;
- is funny, has a sense of humour;
- doesn't send you out crossly;
- only tells you off for serious things like kicking someone, being racist, using a swear word, or talking if it stops others concentrating.

When asked what was the most important out of these qualities, they chose the first two points.

Checklist of approaches which make teaching easier and more rewarding

1. Trust children will work hard, behave well and learn if you have created the appropriate conditions, and always look for what is good.
2. Develop a relationship with each child, understanding how each needs to be treated.
3. Accept all the children unconditionally, even if you do not accept some of their behaviour; make it safe.
4. Match work to a child's ability, needs and *interests*, finding a way to enthuse and inspire.
5. Allow creativity, exploration and play.
6. Recognise that children grow by doing and by being given gradual responsibility which develops independence and autonomous learning.
7. Develop a class code with the children so it is theirs and everyone knows what is expected and how to achieve it.
8. Set boundaries and tasks so that it is easier for children to succeed than fail.
9. Set yourself the task of being *in overall charge of the process* in the classroom rather than trying to *control the children*.

It will be more possible to achieve this with a calm state of mind, a relaxed, centred posture and a confidence in your own authority.

There is a point

When exhausted and feeling overwhelmed by tasks to do and demands to meet it can be easy to forget why on earth you are teaching in the first place. This is usually a time to step back and take a break, even for five minutes. There is a point to it all, even if you cannot recall it at the time. Teachers can have a big impact on the children in their class. Ask any parent.

We may not always be aware of the extent of our influence on the children we teach. However, each new relationship provides the opportunity for helping children develop their own potential a little: kindness, care and sensitivity to who they really are is never wasted. The teacher in Chapter 5 who taught X illustrated this. She touched his life and he was able to be a more fulfilled and confident person as a result, even within the constraints of his great difficulties. As she thought when she saw him two years later and he looked at her and smiled, *'I did have an impact. I did make an impression. You haven't forgotten. It is all there. I did make a difference.'*

This chapter has dealt with:

Developing your own style

- Inner authority
- Trying to be someone else
- Taking on a role model with conviction
- Constructive noise is okay
- Building confidence: developing a relaxed physical presence
- Using your voice
- Considering appearance
- Fostering intuition
- Refining skills

Maintaining motivation

- Finding satisfaction
- Avoiding disaffection: managing stress
- Support system and balance: care for the carers
- Cultivating calm

Summing up

- What the children say
- Checklist of approaches which make teaching easier and more rewarding
- There is a point.

Appendices

A. Specific Learning Difficulties – Signs and symptoms

It is particularly hard for Reception and Infant school teachers to differentiate between children who are developing the many skills and attributes important for successful learning *more slowly* than the norm, from those whose progress is affected by a *developmental learning difficulty*. Later on, in the Junior school, poor attainment may be ascribed to the specific learning difficulties most frequently associated with children's problems in learning to read and write. Specific Language Impairment (SLI) and Attention Deficit/Hyperactivity Disorder (AD/HD) are serious conditions which may be misconstrued.

The purpose here is to provide a brief guide to these disorders, so that the Primary school teacher may be alert to the possibility of specific difficulties which lie outside the range of normal individual differences. Early identification and intervention are crucial if a pattern of increasing 'failure', low self-esteem and distress is to be avoided.

Learning difficulties tend to run in families, and their early signs are usually evident well before school entry. It is important, therefore, to consider preschool development and family background, as well as the results of Baseline Assessment, together with the child's educational progress and adjustment in school, to see if a discernible pattern emerges. It should be noted that there are many 'within-child' and environmental factors which affect educational progress; also, children's rate of development – particularly in the early years – varies considerably. In addition, learning difficulties can co-exist, interact with and compound each other (e.g. dyslexia *and* dyspraxia), so an extract match with the 'textbook' case is not always seen.

The milder learning difficulty may not become evident until the demands of learning to read and write, or use of these skills independently, impose demands on a child with which his or her fragile skills cannot cope. The more severe difficulty will cause concern in school from the start. The informed teacher who is alert to the various possibilities will be in a strong position to distinguish delay, from disorder, from the normal mix, to be expected in any school. In all problem cases, careful checks on eyesight and hearing should not be overlooked.

Dyslexia

In the majority of cases, dyslexics' written language difficulties are rooted in subtle problems with the sound (phonological) system of spoken language. These may manifest themselves to a certain extent in their speech, but the major effect is on the acquisition of phonics and thus encoding/decoding language at the single *word* level. Questions to ask are:

- Is there a history of language/literacy problems within the family (e.g. parents, grandparents, siblings, cousins)?
- Was the child late learning to talk? Was/is the child's speech immature for his or her age, their pronunciation inaccurate or unclear? Has the child ever been referred for Speech and Language Therapy?
- Does the child have trouble with activities based on alliteration and rhyming (which develop phonological awareness) – e.g. learning/joining in with rhymes, playing 'I Spy'?
- Is the child having great difficulty with mastering sound-symbol correspondence – distinguishing between the short vowel sounds (especially *a* from *e*), between 'voiced and unvoiced' consonants (e.g. *p* from *b*, *t* from *d*); letter names from letter sounds?
- Is the child stuck at 'look and say' (or 'look and guess') stage of reading and not able to use phonics effectively to decode words when needed?
- Does child find it difficult to *use* phonics fluently to spell? In their spelling 'bizarre' so that their attempts do not follow the sequence of sounds in the spoken word (e.g. *splich* for ship, *stmck* for mistake). Or, can the child sound out a word and represent each phoneme, even if the spelling is not correct (e.g. *sed* for said; *wokt* for walked; *iskweem* for ice-cream). *Note:* The normally developing child tends to spell by sound and so their attempts are likely to reflect the way he or she speaks, but do appear reasonably logical – if a little unorthodox!
- Is there an uneven profile of attainment – speaking and listening better than reading and writing; maths and science (also technology, art, ICT) better than English?
- Is the child's confidence and self-esteem deteriorating? Does he or she dislike reading, avoid writing activities?

Further information
British Dyslexia Association, 98 London Road, Reading, Berkshire RG1 5AU. Tel: 0118 966 8271.

Recommended reading
Layton, L., Deeny, K. and Upton, G. (1997) *Sound, Practice, Phonological Awareness in the Classroom*. London: David Fulton Publishers.
   The focus of this book is on building good foundations for the acquisiton of literacy skills, during the early years.
Snowling, M. and Stackhouse, J. (1996) *Dyslexia, Speech and Language. A Practitioner's Handbook*. London: Whurr.
   This book includes up-to-date theory about dyslexia and describes successful methods of teaching reading, spelling, writing and handwriting.

Who can help?
Educational Psychologists; Advisory/Specialist SpLD teachers. Speech and language therapists (but only if the literacy problems are rooted in significant speech and language difficulties).
A list of centres offering part-time specialist SpLD teacher training courses is available from: OCR (Oxford, Cambridge and RSA) Examination Board, Westwood Way, Coventry CV4 8HS. Tel: 01203 470033.

Dyspraxia

This is sometimes known as 'clumsy child syndrome' and its main effect on the development of literacy skills is on handwriting. Specific difficulties in *planning and executing a sequence of voluntary movements* may also result in difficulties with speech production, and a range of fine and gross motor skills. The salient questions are:

- Is there a history of delayed development of motor skills at the preschool stage – walking, feeding self, dressing self, etc.?
- Does the child now have poor fine motor skills? Are buttons, zips, buckles, shoelaces, using a knife and fork, problem areas? Does the child find cutting, sticking, drawing, handwriting really difficult?
- What about motor coordination in general – PE, ball skills, riding a bike?
- Is the child extremely impractical and disorganised – often does not seem to know where they should be, what they should be doing/have with them?
- Is the child's confidence and self-esteem gradually deteriorating? Are other children getting fed up with them?

Further information
The Dyspraxia Foundation, 8 West Alley, Hitchin, Hertfordshire SG5 1EG. Tel: 01462 454986.

Recommended reading
Ripley, K., Daines, B. and Barrett, J. (1997) *Dyspraxia. A Guide for Teachers and Parents.* London: David Fulton Publishers.

Who can help?
Educational Psychologists; Advisory/Specialist SpLD teachers; Advisory PE teachers; Paediatric Occupational Therapists; Paediatric Physiotherapists; Speech and Language Therapists (if there is *oral* dyspraxia).

Specific Language Impairment (SLI)

The many manifestations of SLI affect *oral* as well as *written* communication and so severely affected children should have been identified well before school entry. However, those with milder problems, perhaps not perceived as such by inexperienced parents, may come to the attention of staff who realise that the child's language skills are deficient. SLI affects a child's social integration, since other children will find talking/playing with them exacting. Educationally, all learning is likely to be affected (although practical subjects less so than English/maths skills). Particular problems at *sentence* and *text* level will be apparent with regard to literacy skills.

What specific indicators might be noted in the context of a history of delayed language development in the preschool years and persisting problems with *understanding* and/or *producing* age-appropriate language? At school, an SLI child may:

- misunderstand/not respond appropriately to questions or instructions; forget what he or she has been told and so copy/follow other children a great deal;
- go off the point, 'all around the houses', get in a muddle and repeat themselves when speaking (or writing); have very limited vocabulary;
- seem to talk at others rather than partake in two-way conversations; lose the thread of conversations;
- have poor *reading comprehension* (although accuracy may be at the expected level);
- have difficulty when speaking and writing in formulating grammatically correct sentences;
- become withdrawn and have few friends.

Further information
AFASIC (Association For All Speech Impaired Children), 69–86 Old Street, London EC1V 9HX. Tel: 0207 841 8900.

Recommended reading
Beveridge, M. and Conti-Ramsden, G. (1987) *Children with Language Disabilities.* Milton Keynes: Open University Press.

A brief and readable guide to normal language development and the various disorders which impact on learning and literacy development.

The AFASIC Checklists and User's Guide (1991) Learning Development Aids.

A useful recourse when considering whether a child should be referred for assessment/advice to a Speech and Language Therapist.

Who can help?
Educational Psychologists; Advisory teachers for Speech and Language; Speech and Language Therapists.

Attention Deficit Disorder (AD/HD)

This is a neurological condition, the symptoms of which, in milder cases, are sometimes confused with the behaviour of the more lively and demanding but 'normal' child. There are three core symptoms

- inattention
- hyperactivity
- impulsivity

present in number and to a degree that seriously affect a child's ability to function.

Inattention. Short attention span/inability to concentrate results in difficulties in learning to speak, motor skills, reading writing, etc.

Hyperactivity. These children are always 'on the go' as if driven by a motor and do not sleep much (and so parents become seriously overtired). At school, they are never in their seats, talk and interrupt continually and cause lots of disruption. Teachers *and* other children become irritated, so they can have problems making/keeping friends. They are often accident-prone.

Impulsivity. The core deficit is thought to be the inability to prevent response to impulse – whether appropriate or inappropriate. Such children cannot seem to stop themselves from responding to either internal or external stimuli (thoughts, feelings/noises, 'happenings'). Their distractibility and disorganisation stems from the primary problem of being *unable to wait;* their difficulty is in *not* responding to whatever is most interesting or rewarding at the moment.

For obvious reasons, they nearly all underachieve at school (20 per cent have reading difficulties and 60 per cent serious handwriting problems).

Further information
ADD Information Services, PO Box 340, Edgware, Middlesex HA8 9HL (send large stamped addressed envelope). Tel: 020 8905 2013.

Recommended reading
Cooper, P. and Ideus, K. (1996) *Attention Deficit/Hyperactivity Disorder. A Practical Guide for Teachers.* London: David Fulton Publishers.
Munden, A. and Arcelus, J. (1999) *The AD/HD Handbook. A Guide for Parents and Professionals on Attention Deficit Hyperactivity Disorder.* London and Philadelphia: Jessica Kingsley Publishers.

Who can help?
Paediatricians; Education/Clinical Psychologists; Advisory/Support teachers for EBD; Advisory/Specialist SpLD teachers. Since this is a medical condition with a huge impact on behaviour and learning, it follows that the treatment team will be multi-professional. Drug therapy in conjunction with behaviour management and learning support it the most effective form of intervention.

© Gill Backhouse, Chartered Psychologist.
Department of Human Communication Science, University College London.

B. Listening Games

These listening games will need to be adapted to fit the age of the pupils you are teaching.

1. Practise playing Chinese whispers in groups of about 10. The teacher could supply pupils with sentences, or they could make up their own on a theme or using certain key words. Talk about how difficult it is sometimes to listen and understand.
2. Read out a short story or passage, or play a tape, asking the children to tick off on a sheet key words or pictures when they hear them.
3. The children work in pairs. One speaks first, talking about a topical issue for the class, something they have just learnt, for example, or about a recent visit. The other pupil listens. Both try to notice if and when the listener's attention wanders. Does he or she move at this point or look away from the speaker? Usually people move their position slightly when they stop listening. How might this information help them stay on track or refocus in the future? Roles are swapped.
4. Again working in pairs, one child describes a picture he or she can see but the partner cannot. It is the partner's task to draw the picture he or she hears described. Roles are then swapped.
5. A group of pupils work together using a tape recorder. They have a bingo card each and listen to the tape which is the 'caller'. The items on the cards could cover a range of subjects, for example, scientific terms, grammar points, times tables, whole sentences, or words to be matched to pictures. If they have the word called out on their card they cover it up. The first person to cover all on their card wins.

C. Games for Learning Spelling

1. *Hangman* using target words. This could be played as a whole-class activity, for a few minutes here and there.
2. *Bingo.*
   (a) The children have a card each bearing a different selection of the target words. There is a pack of word cards which are turned over one at a time. Children cover the word on their bingo card if it appears on a card from the pack.
   (b) An alternative is for a small group of children to work with a tape recorder listening to a tape giving letter sounds. When they hear a letter sound occurring in words on their bingo card they cover it up until all the words are covered.
3. *Word building.*
   a) The children throw two dice. They add the numbers in order to see which letters they can choose. A chart shows which letters can be gained for which numbers, for example, 2 = a, b or c; 3 = d, e or f; 4 = g or h; 5 = i, j or k; 6 = e,l or m; 7 = n or o; 8 = p or q; 9 = r, s or t; 10 = u or v; 11 = w or x; 12 = y

or z. Children then build up the target words using their letters. They have the target words on cards for reference.

(b) As above, except that children gain letters by letter cards being dealt out initially and then by drawing more from a pack in turn.

(c) Fishing. This involves the same word building as above, except that children 'fish' with magnets for letters which can be written on fish-shaped cards with a paper clip.

(d) Children throw a dice and move a counter around a board. Some spaces are letters. When landing on a letter, the player takes this letter from a pool to build a word matching a target word on their card. Landing on some spaces a player misses a turn, has an extra turn, has to return a certain letter or has the opportunity to choose any letter he or she wishes.

The children can make the cards themselves, the teacher giving guidance, for example, helping children write syllables in different colours to aid recognition, underlining vowels. Or older children could make them for younger ones.

4. *Pelmanism.* Pairs of the target words are written, one word on each card. Five or six pairs are then shuffled and placed faced down on a table. Each player picks up two cards at a time and shows them to the other players, the aim being to pick up matching pairs. If they match, the player keeps them, if not he or she replaces them face down. The player with most pairs wins.

5. *Treasure Hunt.* In teams, the children solve clues to find letter cards hidden around the room or, maybe, in the playground. When the team has found all the letters they place them over their target word cards to finish. If one team plays at a time this can help keep order.

D. Games for learning tables

There are a number of games which can be played to practise tables simply by multiplying the numbers on two dice rather than adding them. Dice with up to 12 numbers on them are also available to use once children are confident multiplying by one to six. To learn one table at a time, if special dice are not available, one of the two dice can be altered so that all faces are the same number, that of the table to be practised.

1. Players are each given a copy of the multiplication table to be practised. In turn, they throw two dice, one up to 12, the other showing the number of a times table. They multiply the numbers together and tick off the line on their table. If they threw a 7 and an 8, for example, they would tick $8 \times 7 = 56$. The winner is the player to finish the table first.

2. This game requires 48 cards and two dice prepared as above. The cards are made up of four each of all the products of the multiplication table. For the seven times table, for example, there would be four cards with a 7, four with 14, four with 21, and so on. The game is for two or three players. Children throw the dice, multiply the numbers and pick up the appropriate card. The game continues until all the cards have been picked up. The aim is to collect as many 'families' of four as possible.

3. Bingo can easily be adapted to practise tables. Bingo cards are made up with a selection of the products of the tables to be learnt. Cards bearing the full line of the times table are turned over one at a time and read out. For example, some of the bingo cards might have 27 on them. The card read out would say $3 \times 9 = 27$ or $9 \times 3 = 27$.

E. Games with a newly formed class

Getting to know names

The aim is for pupils to say their own name to the class and to learn the names of some of their classmates.

Pupils sit in a circle. The teacher has a ball the size of an orange made of crinkled silver foil. He or she rolls the ball to someone in the circle saying his or her name. The pupil who receives the ball does the same and so on until all pupils have said their names. The game can be played again, this time the person rolling saying the name of the person to whom he or she is rolling the ball. Pupils may need to repeat their own names from time to time as reminders. The teacher may need to ensure that all receive the ball at some time.

A similar game can be played in a larger space. In this, children stand in a circle. One class member starts by walking around the inside of the circle carrying an interesting item, preferably something light, interesting and robust, for example a beautiful stone or a piece of carved wood. He or she stops in front of a classmate and hands it over to him or her. The new carrier says, *'Thank you. My name is . . .'* and then repeats the process. The game can be played another time with the first person being thanked by name, *'Thank you . . . My name is . . .'*.

This game not only helps pupils learn names but it also affords the opportunity for eye contact and social skills to be practised.

Another game to be played in a large space is as follows. The teacher shows the children three or four bases. These might be the walls of the room or other clearly designated separate areas. The teacher then asks all the children wearing a certain colour to walk to one base, those wearing another colour to go to the second base and so on. Children wearing two or more of the colours mentioned go to the first colour called out. When at their bases the children have to get into a circle *without speaking*. Once in their circle the teacher says who goes first in each group. The pupils then have to say their names in turn so everyone in their group can hear. When they have done this in one direction they repeat it in the other. The pupils then walk quietly back to the central area and await the next instruction. Another way of selecting the groups might be hair colour, eye colour, birthday in a certain month, and so on.

This is quite a demanding game and the pupils might find it difficult at first and some will need considerable help deciding where to go, forming a circle and speaking in turn. Persevering amid chaos can be worthwhile since it practises a number of collaborative skills. It can also be adapted later in other ways: as a basis for working on bar charts; to practise letter sounds and awareness, children going into groups depending on initial letter sounds in their names, numbers of letters in their names. It can also be used as a stimulus for discussing differences within the class.

F. Instructions for the peace table

Goldfish

1. *Tell the other person*
- how you feel *(I feel . . . . .)*
- how things looked to you *(It looked to me as if . . . . .)*
- how things sounded to you *(It sounded to me as if . . . . .)*
- what you were trying to do *(I was just trying to . . . . .)*

2. *Listen to the other person (no interrupting)*
- Imagine you are in his or her shoes.
- What does it feel like?
- How do things look and sound from his or her shoes?

3. *Has there been a misunderstanding?*
4. *Do you want to say anything else? Does the other person want to? If so, listen.*
5. *Can you two say anything to sort things out?*
6. *Do you need a teacher or other adult to help you now?*

Budgie

This is the same except that points 1 and 2 are reversed.

Bibliography

Ayers, H., Clarke, D. and Murray, A. (2000) *Perspectives on Behaviour*, 2nd Ed. London: David Fulton Publishers.

Bandler, R. and Grinder, J. (1979) *Frogs into Princes*. Utah: Real People Press.

Benson, P. and Martin, P. (1999) *Design for a Life*. London: Cape.

Bentley, T. (1998) *Learning Beyond the Classroom*. London: Routledge.

Beveridge, M. and Conti-Ramsden, G. (1987) *Children with Language Disabilities*. Milton Keynes: Open University Press.

Black, P. and William, D. (1998) *Inside the Black Box*. London: King's College.

Bradshaw, J. (1988) *Bradshaw on: THE FAMILY*. Florida: Health Communications Inc.

Bruce, T. (1987) *Early Childhood Education*. London: Hodder and Stoughton.

Castle, E. B. (1961) *Ancient Education and Today*. Harmondsworth: Penguin.

Cooper, P. and Ideus, K. (1996) *Attention Deficit/Hyperactivity Disorder: A practical guide for teachers*. London: David Fulton Publishers.

Cowie, H. and Sharp, S. (1996) *Peer Counselling in Schools: A time to listen*. London: David Fulton Publishers.

Deming, W. Edwards (1994) *New Economics for Industry, Government and Education*. Boston, Mass.: Massachusetts Institute of Technology.

Diener, E. *et al.* (1978) 'An analysis of learned helplessness: continuous change in performance, strategy and achievement cognitions after failure', *Journal of Personality and Social Psychology* **36**, 451–62.

Docking, J. (1990) *Managing Behaviour in the Primary School*. London: David Fulton Publishers.

Fontana, D. and Slack, I. (1997) *Teaching Meditation to Children*. Shaftesbury, Dorset: Element.

Galbraith, P. (1997) *Meditate Rejuvenate*. Singapore: Media Masters.

Gardner, H. (1983) *Frames of Mind*. London: Fontana.

Gardner, H. (1991) *The Unschooled Mind: How children think and how schools should teach*. New York: Basic Books.

Goleman, D. (1996) *Emotional Intelligence: Why it can matter more than IQ*. London: Bloomsbury.

Gray, F. (1974) 'Little brother is changing you', *Psychology Today*, March.

James, O. (1998) *Britain on the Couch*. London: Arrow Books.

Keele University Centre for Successful Schools (1994) *Young People and Their*

Attitudes to School. Interim report. Keele: Keele University.

Latzko, W. J. (1997) 'Modeling the Method. The Deming Classroom', *Quality in Management Journal* 97.

Layton, L., Deeny, K. and Upton, G. (1997) *Sound Practice: Phonological awareness in the classroom.* London: David Fulton Publishers.

Le Shan, L. (1995) *How to Meditate.* London: Thorsons.

MacGilchrist, B., Myers, K. and Reed, J. (1997) *The Intelligent School.* London: Sage.

Mann, D. (1997) *Psychotherapy: an Erotic Relationship.* London: Routledge.

Marland, M. (1975) *The Craft of the Classroom.* London: Heinemann.

Mash, H. W., *et al* (1984) 'Determinants of students' self concept: is it better to be a relatively large fish in a small pond even if you don't learn to swim well?' *Journal of Personality and Social Psychology* 47 213–31.

McNamara, E. (1999) *Positive Pupil Management and Motivation.* London: David Fulton Publishers.

Miller, A. (1983) *For your own Good (The Roots of Violence in Child-rearing).* London: Faber and Faber.

Moir, A. and Moir, W. (1998) *Why Men Don't Iron.* London: HarperCollins.

Mosley, J. (1994) *Turn your School Around.* Wisbech: Learning Development Aids.

Munden, A. and Arcelus, J. (1999) *The AD/HD Handbook. A guide for parents and professionals on Attention Deficit Hyperactivity Disorder.* London and Philadelphia: Jessica Kingsley Publishers.

Orbach, S. (1999) *Towards Emotional Literacy.* London: Virago Press.

Ott, P. (1997) *How to Detect and Manage Dyslexia.* London: Heinemann.

Perkins, D. (1995) *Outsmarting IQ.* New York: Free Press.

Phillips, A. (1998) *The Beast in the Nursery.* London: Faber and Faber.

Quinn, K. (1983) *Stand Your Ground.* London: Orbis Publishing.

Ripley, K., Daines, B. and Barrett, J. (1997) *Dyspraxia: A guide for teachers and parents.* London: David Fulton Publishers.

Robertson, J. (1981) *Effective Classroom Control.* London: Hodder and Stoughton.

Ryan, K. and Oestreich, D. K. (1991) *Driving Fear out of the Workplace.* San Francisco: Jossey Bass.

Salovey, P. and Mayer, J. D. (1990) 'Emotional Intelligence', *Imagination, Cognition and Personality* 9, 185–211.

Salzberger-Wittenberg, I., Henry, G. and Osborn E. (1983) *The Emotional Experience of Learning and Teaching.* London: Routledge and Kegan Paul.

Snowling, M. and Stackhouse, J. (1996) *Dyslexia, Speech and Language. A practioners handbook.* London: Whurr.

Selye, H. (1976) *The Stress of Life*, revised edition. New York: McGraw-Hill.

Wilhelm, H. (1989) *Tyrone the Horrible.* London: Scholastic Publications (first published New York 1988).

Winnicott, D. W. (1958) 'The Antisocial Tendency', in *Collected Papers: Through Paediatrics to Psycho-Analysis.* London: Tavistock Publications.

Yogananda Paramahansa (1953) *Autobiography of a Yogi.* Los Angeles: Self-realization Fellowship.

Yogananda Paramahansa (1999) *Inner Peace.* Los Angeles: Self-realization Fellowship.

Zeldin, T. (1998) *Conversation.* London: Harvill Press.

Index

Printed in the United Kingdom
by Lightning Source UK Ltd.
123626UK00007B/27-36/A